My Roots, My People

First Edition.
Paperback ISBN # 978-0-939927-32-6
Library of Congress Control Number: 2024947694

The book's title, *My Roots, My People* is a line from the poem in this anthology entitled "Olive Tree" by Jack Byrett.

Cover Artist: Leo Simmons

California Poets in the Schools
P.O. Box 1328, Santa Rosa, CA 95402
415-221-4201
info@cpits.org
https://www.californiapoets.org

Meg Hamill, Executive Director
David Sibbet, President of the Board

California Poets IN THE SCHOOLS

My Roots, My People

2023-2024
California Poets in the Schools
60th Anniversary Statewide Anthology

California Poets in the Schools
Santa Rosa

In memory of Maureen Hurley,
who ignited a creative spark in thousands of youth in
her too-short time on Earth.

Foreword

Welcome to the 60th Anniversary Youth Poetry Anthology of California Poets in the Schools.

Take your time with these poems. Savor them. You might read them more than once. Your reaction—whether delight, astonishment, or something else, may come out from the same or different places each time.

Poetry writing isn't easy. Some of us might have just forgotten how, as William Stafford might have said. All the same, neither is learning how to dance or walk or tie a shoelace or use a fork or use chopsticks or how to sing. But each of these writers have tried and failed and tried and failed and tried. Now we have this volume, the latest in a long series of anthologies from California Poets in the Schools, which started sixty years ago.

Are we making sense in a poem? No, but yes. Is the poem precise and detailed? Yes, but in the end, no, because those details only expand and seed the garden of your own heart. Is there music in the poem? Yes, but not necessarily a melody you know, so listen carefully, very carefully. You might have to find it by saying it aloud, or you might have to listen in silence. Be gentle and generous with yourself.

What are the elements these students use to write their poems? First, they had time to sit down and to be still and silent. They had classroom teachers and poet teachers who encouraged them to be brave, courageous and trusting enough to put their pencils to paper and try to find the right words, words which traveled from out there or in their hearts and inside their bodies, into their arms, through their hands, fingers, and pencils, onto the page. What came out was something often messy and awkward and which eventually grew and got shaped, re-shaped, edited, and became the poems you see here.

Also important was listening to each other and to the poems we put before them. We poet teachers have often guided the students by showing them poems that someone else wrote. What did people notice? What did they hear? What did any poem make them feel or think about? Did it inspire them?

Sometimes we say poetry writing is magic or inspired. I want to say that poem writing is a lot of work. There's no going around the work. No one knows the work behind the poems. The students discover that work by trying to write their own poems.

We ask the students to read poems aloud—they themselves read, and we help them if needed. Sometimes we show students one of our own poems or the story of that poem. For any poem, we ask, what did this poem do with its words? Was one language enough? Did the poem make up words that didn't exist before? Is that allowed? What is this poem about? What started this poem? Do you think it was hard to write it? Why? Did it play around with word sounds, did it get carried away? If yes, did it swim back from a poetic rip tide of words, or did it keep going? Did the poem make sense? Did it have to? What are we talking about when we say sense? Did you listen enough to remember that poem?

And to the person who asks, can I write about this, is it OKAY to do something not quite....? Our reaction, if you were to call it that, is to ask, whose poem is this? It is, of course, theirs, and now it is yours, reader.

So read these poems. See what happens. Do they tickle, astonish, depress or delight? If you read them aloud, does their sound change your impression? If the writer herself reads her own poem aloud, what is your reaction? What did you hear and remember? When you read or heard them, did something open up, a feather on the ground?

Daryl Ngee Chinn
Poet-Teacher
Board President Emeritus, California Poets in the Schools
Arcata, California

In memory of Maureen Hurley,
John Oliver Simon, and Susan Sibbet

Table of Contents

Colors and Sounds
of Our World

Colors in the World

I see color every day
in our big beautiful world
Black is the color of death
The feeling you get when your life
feels like a landslide
Black is the color you see
when you close your eyes and dream
The time you're asleep but yet most awake
When you have the most imagination
in your marvelous magical mind
Black is sort of related to love
but quite the opposite
Black is the color of heartbreak
When someone that you think you love or trust
betrays you or hurts you
Black is the color of the night sky alongside shining stars

Yellow is the color of joy
That feeling when you are
having fun with your friends
Yellow is the color of the sun
when it's time to start your day
Yellow is the color of laughter
When you feel like one thousand bubbles
are popping in your mouth
Or when you think you are going to cry
but you do quite the opposite
Yellow is the color of lemons, like life they are
Sour at the beginning but sweet at the end

Green is the color of disgust
The feeling when you don't enjoy or like something
Green is the color of nature, grass or leaves
When you think of nature,
you think of the color green like a Granny Smith
Green is the color of an alligator swimming in a lake
Waiting to attack, hunting for its next victim
Green is the color of nuclear toxicity
Green is the color of war
People in the military risk their lives to save our country
Dressed in the color green like their surroundings

Red is the color of love
Not controllable but feels good when you find the right person
but bad when they make you broken inside
Red is the color of anger even fury
The feeling when you want to hurt someone
Red is the color of blood
Inside your body and always a part of you
Red is the color of a phoenix

Phoenix means rebirth or rising and emerging from the ashes
Which is what people should do - never back down never give up

Phoenix Pointer, Grade 5
Lu Sutton Elementary, Marin County
Pamela Stuzman, Classroom Teacher
Michele Rivers, Poet Teacher

Red

Red is an octopus
pushing its way through the water.

Red is chewing licorice
while watching a movie.

Red is a crab clicking its claws,
click click, click click.

Red is a group of snakes
Slithering through the trees.

Red is anger
when I do something wrong.

Jackson Olson, Grade 3
Pleasant Valley Elementary, Marin County
Elizabeth Arnold, Classroom Teacher
Lea Aschkenas, Poet Teacher

The History of Color

One day a girl asked an artist   what the color
of insanity was   and his first thought
was to paint the hue
of her skin.
     On some   delicate planes
she was a pink   one breath
away from white, a wound bleeding
invisibly.
          (She called it peach.) Still other
curves she named with the calligraphy
of liquid metal.
          (bronze. copper. gold.) These
were the places he chose   to bury
his fingers in,
     flesh to the knuckle,   and pull—
seams cracking bloodlessly.
the human equivalent
     of yellowed glaze.   Underneath
her claim   on the orange spectrum
he found
     sinew and muscle cells   sketching
their signature.   all over her prison-bars
     of a body, baptizing
the bones *bleach-white,*
          (a brush of tan.) And still,
he pulled. The melanin canvas   stretched
over her profile,   strained
to fit her christening.
          (at last,)   She gave out,
ribcage bared like a grimace,
     center opened to his eyes.
Her names scattered.   like scales.

Instead of a heart   lived
a fleshy ouroboros   swallowing
itself in a fit   of crimson and blue,   a palette
of blood in all
     its forms of breathing.
These shades he   never called
by name,   but rather what
they could be made from:
     the scouring of
her body,   turpentine, clean pages.
First the words,
     then the source.   Her lips
  were the last to go, the satire
of speech.
all that was left   was some color
     defined purely by
the warmth of its lighting,
its reflection of the world, some
     bloody being,   beating
into itself,   over,
               over again.

Clarisse Kim, Grade 11
Abraham Lincoln High School, Marin County
Deeana Datangel, Classroom Teacher
Maxine Flasher-Düzgüneş, Poet Teacher

Black

You bring the black in me
The shimmering night sky in me
The cat that runs through the street
The beautiful tuxedo at a party
The French beret of an artist
The crying mime trapped in a box
The night sky with all the twinkling stars
The clothes you wear at a funeral
I am there

Cy Aridio Perego-Saldana, Grade 3
Montecito Union Elementary, Santa Barbara County
Lisa Monson, Classroom Teacher
Kimbrough Ernest, Poet Teacher

The Colors of Happiness

My soul wants the color of happiness,
love and joy filling me up.
My soul is not afraid of darkness.
My soul is strong, it dreams
of no more sadness left in the world.
My soul wishes to help,
to save all those in need.
My soul wants to feed the poor.
My soul wants to travel to the island of joy.

Valentina Saini, Grade 4
Alexander Valley Elementary, Sonoma County
Nadia Podesto, Classroom Teacher
Maureen Hurley, Poet Teacher

Violet

Oh violet, you smell like my garden,
a mix of sweetness and earthiness.
You taste like burnt cookies,
sweet but bitter.
You are calm like the waves
crashing on the shore.
You sound like the wind,
ferocious but quiet.
You look like the bud of a peach tree.
You feel like a stream,
smoothing a rock
You are sadness, you are hope.
You are past, you are future.
You are beautiful and I love you.

Madison Keats, Grade 3
Vallecito Elementary, Marin County
Dara Ferra, Classroom Teacher
Terri Glass, Poet Teacher

Pink

Pink skips between the cherry blossoms by
the glistening lake full of koi fish. Her father,
the closest blossom to the lake, her mother, the
sunset of exploding colors that sinks into the
lake each night. She plays her violin like a bird
singing softly in the early morning. She loves
swimming in the lake near where she was born.
Sometimes, she wanders in the streets of Japan
near the lake. She treats the cherry blossoms to
help them bloom. Pink.

Calvino Di Loreto, Grade 4
Montecito Union School, Santa Barbara County
Shannon Gallup, Classroom Teacher
Cie Gumucio, Poet Teacher

Sounds Of Our World

Silence is the exhale after a busy long day of labor.
Loudness is the pounding of determined feet on a racetrack
Silence is a heartbeat singing to the soft melody on the radio.
Loudness is the sound of hatred and manmade weapons that
disrupt the peace and shatter millions.
Silence is the golden sun that lights up the night sky like a candle.

Silence is the sound of the soft breeze
that glides through the morning sky.
Loudness is the raging ocean that flows
upon command of the moon.
Silence is the gaze upon the night sky
where restless stars paint an endless abyss.
Loudness is the heart of a fearless lion as he stands,
mighty in his position as king.
Loudness is the sound of a blazing wildfire,
brighter than the midnight stars while
polluting the world with blackness.

Silence is the decaying of stone that tells stories of the past,
long forgotten.
Loudness is the sound of falling civilizations that made
up our world for as long as we can remember.
Silence is the ocean of our great blue sky
that no artist can perfectly replicate.

Silence is a smooth pencil traveling across paper.
Loudness is like the grinding of a pencil sharpener
as it restores a point.
Silence is the soft, silky lead that is rich with words,
pictures, or poetry,
worthless but made of gold.
Silent poetry is like the endless space

that makes up the night sky,
a cocoon ready to be reborn.
Silence is the smooth sweet melodies
and the loudness of determination
that lays deep within our souls.
The sounds that make up our imperfect world.

Cameron Vitasa, 6th Grade
Mill Valley Middle School, Marin County
Juliet Mohit, Classroom Teacher
Michele Rivers, Poet Teacher

I Am the Color Black

My superpower comes from the strength of a raccoon
My magic wand is a book
When you are lost and tired at the tip of an iceberg,
I will become a helicopter to fly you home
When you can't find your parents
I'll stay with you and help as much as I can
When you need to score the winning goal in soccer,
I will cheer you on
When you are sick I will become a blanket
to keep you warm
When you are sad I will be a friend
to make you happy
I am the color Black
I will always
Be behind
Your Back

Jack Hanson, Grade 3
Mountain View Elementary, Santa Barbara County
Holly Bosse, Classroom Teacher
Cie Gumucio, Poet Teacher

Purple

Purple is a butterfly
sitting in a tree.

Purple is a flower
blooming in the summer.

Purple is a t-shirt,
soft and cozy.

Purple is the feeling of sadness
when I miss my mom.

Purple is a dragon fruit,
sweet and juicy.

Purple is a stuffed animal,
soft and cuddly.

Ashly Caballeros, Grade 3
Pleasant Valley Elementary, Marin County
Carolyn Tagliaferri, Classroom Teacher
Lea Aschkenas, Poet Teacher

Nature and the World Around Us

Panthers

Big black panthers running
gracefully in the wind. Light
violet skies over their heads.
An eagle sways in the sky
watching them out of its blue eyes.
A mouse pokes its head out of the ground
and watches too.

Elihu Bogan, Grade 3
Montecito Union Elementary, Santa Barbara County
Kathy Trent, Classroom Teacher
Kimbrough Ernest, Poet Teacher

Here on Planet Earth

Here on planet Earth, we imagine beyond the stars. We have
friendships as strong as the mountains. We wonder to the moon.
We are growing like trees. We tell stories to mother nature. We see
flowers bloom. We listen to birds singing. We hear waves crashing
on the sandy beach. We hear kids laughing. We see animals playing.
We dance and sing. Here on the Earth would be a lot better if we had
peace with others, no homeless people or animals. Here on planet
Earth, we see love in everyone.

Haley Klan, Grade 4
Montecito Union Elementary, Santa Barbara County
Shannon Gallup, Classroom Teacher
Cie Gumucio, Poet Teacher

Dear Earth

Dear Earth,
I love you in the summer,
sky clear and blue,
fruits ripe and sweet,
water cool and relaxing
I love you in the spring,
flowers blooming and growing,
animals being born,
weather both warm and cool
I love you in the autumn,
leaves turning brown and falling,
weather cool and crisp,
animals getting ready for the big sleep
I love you in the winter,
snow falling and glistening
in the heatless sun,
animals asleep
with their bellies full,
days shortening
and nights getting longer,
Earth, I love you

Serenity O'Brien, Grade 6
Cobb Elementary, Lake County
Laurel Phillips, Classroom Teacher
Michele Krueger, Poet Teacher

Ferns

Listen up and settle down
Thousands of leaves making a fern,
like hundreds of campers making a camp.
As we gather around the campfire,
take a look around and see if you can notice them on the
ground
Some are vibrant green, that catches your eyes
Some are as tall as the steam
that comes from my grandma's pumpkin pie.
Ferns that help me stay calm in my mind,
the way they blend into each other,
like campers sinking into their beds.
Majestically living with each other, underneath the Sequoya shade.
Let's remember to forgive ourselves
for not giving the smaller things in life a bigger picture.

Carter Glasspoole, Grade 5
Loma Vista Elementary, Ventura County
Laura Cohn, Classroom Teacher
Vincent Jimenez, Poet Teacher

Dark pink glowing feathering gills sway
in the gentle water.

Diving deeper to the thick, soft sand.
Lily pad shadows create circles of shade.

Cool water flows swooshes past,
small dots of silvery blue race past.
Long lotus stems firm tightly to the ground.

Your shimmering blue eyes follow the bubbles
that float to the surface and pop like bubble gum.

A small silver fish swam around
not knowing that he is about to be
Lunch!

Closer...closer...until he is snapped
into the jaws of a long pink creature.

No fish is a match
for this creature!

Izzy Tahouri, Grade 4
Montecito Union Elementary, Santa Barbara County
Heather Bruski, Classroom Teacher
Cie Gumucio, Poet Teacher

Dandelion

The seeds of a dandelion–
Not the seeds of a weed–
They spread amongst the world,
Carried by the wind into
Myriad backyards, and
City parks, and
Through windows. And
Many skies, and faces
Of the moon, they've seen.
The wind on which they ride
Originates from the pursed,
Angry lips of those
That wish to blow the dandelion away.
The pursed lips whistle
A sour goodbye note
To uproot them into
A sky-melody. The lips
Wish that more wishes be made,
And more seeds of the dandelion
Be blown astray.
These seeds, where they've
Started matters not.
It's where they've gone,
And who they've brushed past,
And what flowers they've planted–
Flowers! for who are you
To call a dandelion a weed?

Some say the wind is a devil,
Stirring up dust and uprooting homes;
But the music of the wind
Is the notes of angelsong–
God's voice, as if

Spoken through a flute.
The seeds beg for motion.
And, though mourning comes with leaving,
Nothing is lost.
Eternity through progeny is gained.
These resilient seeds,
They belong to the world,
Carried by the wind
Into the soils of Gaia.
Lift up this green carpet:

You'll see a Pangaea-network
Of roots interwoven.

O, fields of Virginia flowers;
O, forest meadows of Maryland trees:
You *litter* the nation;
You envelop the Earth.
Domineering you are,
Weeding me out.
If the ground belongs to *you*,
Then the sky belongs to *me*.
God's crescendo carries me
High above and I look down,
Seeking sanctuary;
There is yet soil set aside for me,
There among the trees
Down in California.

Where, O weeping willow tree,
Did you start?
What lips have blown you
With the wind of a wish?
And whose cheek have you caressed?
Through whose window
Did you fly, and

Where were you dropped
Into the soil?
Look down:
Your stem is your roots,
And they've yet to move.
Where are the seeds of a dandelion?
Look up:
They are carried through the staves of angelsong.
The diaspora of your
Flowers is focused–
See *everywhere*
The fruits of a dandelion;
For who are you
To call a dandelion a weed?

Konnor James, Grade 11
Adolfo Camarillo High School, Ventura County
Heidi Resnik, Classroom Teacher
Fernando Salinas, Poet Teacher

The Sadness of Rain

Rain is sadness and fear.
Rain is pressure, pushing you
out of your comfort zone.
Rain is the lakes and rivers
flooding everything, even your heart.
Rain is the sun crying
because the world is not at peace.
Rain is war. But not always.

Emilia Hawley, Grade 4
Alexander Valley Elementary, Sonoma County
Nadia Podesto, Classroom Teacher
Maureen Hurley, Poet Teacher

The Beauty of Nature

A songbird tweets like a melody in the wind
like a soft song. It chirps from the nest
as brown as bark wood that shines
against the sun's rays like a tree
that glows in the day. The birdsong
is the mother as she sings to her babies
like a band singing a soft melody.
She protects her babies like a knight
in shining armor like the protector
of the seven seas. She is there for her
babies and will protect them at all costs
like mother nature protects her babies.
The baby birds begin to grow
like they were born yesterday
as the mother teaches her babies how
to be free to fly like the wind whooshing
through nature like the trees flowing
in the beauty of the hot sun
that shines upon us.

Lola Auriti, Grade 4
Edna McGuire Elementary, Marin County
Sasha Vargas and Katie Ward, Classroom Teachers
Claire Blotter, Poet Teacher

Butterfly Cry

I am a butterfly
I flutter easily through the sky
on soft, silky wings full of color
looking for a place to lay my eggs
but there are no flowers
no plants
no trees, no food, no forest
just empty, bare ground
I feel the strength draining out of me
and I fall down
for an eternal rest
I feel quite sad in my last moments
my children will never see the world
that I had once lived in
I flick my antennae one last time
and fall into an eternal slumber

Hannah Thompson, Grade 5
Cobb Elementary, Lake County
Natasha McKenney, Classroom Teacher
Michele Krueger, Poet Teacher

Mythical, Marvelous, Magical

I glance down at the ground
Mysterious eyes flash back at me
They remind me of a crystal, amethyst, maybe
Sparkling like two lone stars in the night sky
I am mesmerized, the eyes are unblinkingly beautiful
Mythical, marvelous, magical
A small round body stays motionless
Not dead, nor asleep, just peacefully being
I admire the serenity of this moment
The wind rustles through the tall oaks like
Mother nature whispering her quiet secrets to the world
Mythical, marvelous, magical
I reach down and grasp at the cold clean air
As I lay my hand on the dirt, as dark as coal
He crawls into my palm and I feel myself
Rising into the air
I am a beautiful bird, gracefully lifting,
Drifting through the night sky
My hair flows freely in the wind
The moon, the stars, all flash by
It feels like a dream
Mythical, marvelous, magical
He feels soft, like a kiss
The ground is cold under my bare feet
I look for him but he is gone
drifting back into my imagination
Mythical, marvelous, magical

Anna Neto, Grade 5
Nicasio Elementary, Marin County
Megan Young, Classroom Teacher
Michele Rivers, Poet Teacher

The Museum of the Ocean

Giant whales as big as buses
swimming along a massive man-made reef
Eels swinging their tails like trees dancing in the wind
Parrotfish eating at a buffet of coral and seagrass
Sharks with teeth as sharp as knives
eating as many fish as they want
Squids slipping through small cracks
like soap slipping down a drain
Sea urchins staying near rocks
as pointy as a thousand spears
This is the Museum of the Ocean

Tyler Mindigo, Grade 4
Strawberry Point School, Marin County
Lulu Monti, Classroom Teacher
Terri Glass, Poet Teacher

Spring Haiku

after Issa

In hazy spring mist
I will go in the forest
Campfire for the heat

Student Group Poem, Grades 2/3 (combined)
Coleman Elementary, Marin County
Joy Conway, Classroom Teacher
Virginia Barrett, Poet Teacher

Alphabet Poem, A-E: Miwok

A is for acorn,
something to eat
once they're leached.

B is for bolas,
used to catch birds
with rope made of sinew.

C is for collecting,
acorns, buckeye seeds,
fish eggs, huckleberries,
in woven tule baskets.

D is for dome-shaped wigwams
of willow poles and
bundles of tule grass.

E is for experts
in hunting and weaving;
for eagles and elk who lived
in the woods.

Student Group Poem, Grade 3
Venetia Valley School, Marin County
Matthew Pope, Classroom Teacher
Virginia Barrett, Poet Teacher

Secrets of the World

The red fox is in me.
    She taught me where to go and when to stay.
The galaxy is in me.
    It taught me how to learn,
and that I am much more than myself.
    The wind is in me.
He taught me that song is the best breath, and life is movement.
    The ground is in me.
She taught me that living is more than existence.
    My soul is in me.
I taught me how to love, and how to close my eyes.

Kaya Goff, Grade 6
Whitethorn Elementary School, Humboldt
Blair Soffe, Classroom Teacher
Dan Zev Levinson, Poet Teacher

City Underwater

People rushing past
People all around
Tap, tap, tap, as feet hit the ground.
Chattering conversations being carried by the wind.
Bikers passing by like schools of fish,
Clack! Go their pedals, round and round.
Doors clanging open and closed
From crowded cafes,
Like anemones unfolding to greet the salty sea.
Pigeons pecking at crumbs left on the floor.
Fountains spraying water,
Like waves hitting the shore.
Popping bubbles being blown,
Glinting in the light.
Dirt being kicked
Like sand flying in the air.
So many people,
Like streams flowing through.
Roses blooming along the sidewalk
Like colorful coral on the seafloor.
The sun shines brightly,
Spreading its warmth onto others
Like the sun spreads its reflection onto the surface of the sea.
Then you are underwater
Floating and floating
Through the abyss....

Soe Bender, Grade 4
Vieja Valley Elementary, Santa Barbara County
Tairy Birkley, Classroom Teacher
Cie Gumucio, Poet Teacher

Here On Earth

Here on Earth from our oceans to mountains and valleys to deserts, we are incredible in many ways. Humans and animals, women and men, nature and peace are all a part of this world. Our waters spread the Earth and makes up 70 percent of our world. Does your place have as much water or as little land? It gets hot and cold, dark and bright and we see the stars at night. We have friends, family and loved ones everywhere. Life here on Earth would be better if everything was fair. This is Earth and we also have so much more. We are 7 continents and are united as one.

Celine Ley, Grade 4
Montecito Union School, Santa Barbara County
Shannon Gallup, Classroom Teacher
Cie Gumucio, Poet Teacher

At the Beach

I remember when I went to a beach,
There was a baby seal;
It looked lost.
Then it wasn't moving.
Everyone came to see it,
Taking pictures.
It was a nice beach too,
With all types of stores and food to eat;
And a place to swim.

Immanuel Garcia, Grade 8
San Fernando Middle School, Los Angeles County
David Malley, Classroom Teacher
Juan Cardenas, Poet Teacher

Milky Way

I am the luminescent silver
glowing faintly in the vast universe.
I am the spring rain that
lands softly on the trees.
I wish I were the northern
lights shining smoothly and
iridescent in the bright constellations.
I am a cluster of life.
I am the stars when they
are ready to form.
I am the moon when it shines
brightly on the Earth.
I used to be a cloud
drifting in the ocean blue sky.
I used to be a speck of dust
on the busy streets of New York.
But now I am a bromeliad
growing in the botanical
garden in San Francisco's Golden Gate Park.
I am now a jumble of
dust and stars in this diverse world.
And when you look closely, you can see me
the faint flow of the Milky Way.

Nathan Choy, Grade 5
West Portal Elementary, San Francisco County
Marina DeGroot, Classroom Teacher
Susan Terence, Poetry Teacher

Honoring Others

If I Could...

If I could go back
to those days when I thought
the world was butterflies and rainbows
I would.
If I could be back with my best friend
hanging out in our favorite spot
looking out into the midnight sky
not having a care in the world.
If I could go back into time
and share those memories one last time
I can still hang out with him but now
I have to look into the sky to talk to him.
Imagine the stories he could tell.

Alexia Jarquin Samiento, Grade 5
Roseland Elementary, Sonoma County
Garrett Cuneo, Classroom Teacher
Lisa Shulman, Poet Teacher

Sleepy Sunflower

Inside my heart
is my cat, Cookie.
She is light gray
like a cloudy day.

Her yellow eyes are
as colorful as a sunflower.
She sleeps in my bed a lot.

Michelle Reyes, Grade 4
Logan Memorial Educational Campus, San Diego County
Elizabeth Cullen, Classroom Teacher
Johnnierenee Nelson, Poet Teacher

The Door to My Brother

My quest has begun at the dawn,
the first door flies out I step inside and
land on a colorful beach full of magnificent fish

I dance a beautiful dance that summons the sun then I go
                    Down
          Down
               Down to get to the next door decorated with gems

When I swim through the next door
I land in a kitchen and the task
is to teach people how to cook

I get everything ready then BAM
I am in an evergreen forest

I make a basket out of red,
orange and yellow flowers hand woven and
hope he will enjoy it with all his heart

The next door is emotional it has
pictures of my birth parents and my
siblings, how much I want my parents but it's too late

And finally
the door that I've been waiting for my whole life
My brother's door and it's decorated
with all his favorite things

I started to cry tears of joy because
it's the first time I've ever met him

Chloe Confiac, Grade 5
Mountain View Elementary, Santa Barbara County
Nate Latta, Classroom Teacher
Cie Gumucio, Poet Teacher

My Bulldog, Truly

Inside my heart
is my puppy named Truly,
small as a baby
brown and white
like hot chocolate.

Her favorite toy to chew on
is a squeaky, furry chick,
gray as a storm.

Mia Garnica, Grade 4
Logan Memorial Educational Campus, San Diego County
Elizabeth Cullen, Classroom Teacher
Johnnierenee Nelson, Poet Teacher

Angel Island Immigrants

(imagining the plight of detainees held at Angel Island 1910-1940)

Outside I see the winds blowing the waves
onto the land of the free
Sometimes I wonder if it is the land of the free
I hear the knives carving text in the walls
Inside I see the stone hard beds and rip't sheets
I miss the smell of outside and freedom
I remember the flowers and bushes or a garden
I feel like a prisoner that has a lifetime sentence of jail
Living at Angel Island is like living in jail
I wish that that I could go to the land of the free

Soham Parikh Rayham, Grade 3
Francis Scott Key Elementary, San Francisco County
Ryan Van Arkel, Classroom Teacher
Susan Terence, Poet Teacher

Love Lines

The rain feels like gentle waves.
I am a star shining brightly with the moon.
Pink will always be my color no matter what.
Streets are cracking like how my heart did
when my loved ones passed away.
I see my special Abby smiling at me
with her cute chubby cheeks.
I am Sojourner Truth.
I love I love
My poems
My poems
I love
All these
poems.

Jazlyn Villanueva, Grade 3
Chenoweth Elementary, Merced County
Amy Brown, Classroom Teacher
Dawn Trook, Poet Teacher

Mirror Image

Lexi, with eyes that shift
from brown to green in warm sunlight.
Her hair the color of a dry,
brown mountain hugging the bright, blue sky.
Lexi, the protector and guardian of her big sister,
who fight together
against epilepsy.
Her imagination and creativity
soar in the sky like a stray balloon.
Lexi, the funny girl who can send a ripple of giggles.
Her growth mindset grows beyond limits
like a big willow tree.
Lexi, who has a voice of a lion
when it comes to writing.
Her personality stretches out
when music is played.
Lexi, and her love for animals is
sometimes stronger than her love for humans.
Her hands go as fast as a cheetah
when you give her a pencil and paper.
And how her eyes glisten in art class.
Lexi, whose heart loosens when
swimming in Jamaican waters—
everything there is medicine.
Her ears that are often listening to Taylor Swift.
Her hopes and dreams to someday become an artist
are as strong as a gorilla pounding on its chest.
Her self-confidence seems dull but has a teeny shine.

Lexi, who constantly tries
to keep that little self-confidence light on.
Her pride reaches for the sky's rainbow after a cool rain.

Lexi Lang-Heaven, Grade 5
Strawberry Point School, Marin County
Daniel Gasparini, Classroom Teacher
Terri Glass, Poet Teacher

The Land with No Summer

Prologue: This poem is about my Japanese great-great-grandfather,
who was sent to Siberia after WWII.

I picked up the rusted shovel
With my cold, blistered hands
In the land where summer does not exist
I was the undertaker of one of my dead companions
I was the one
Who buried him with freezing snow instead of dirt
No coffin
No flowers
The gravestone being a tiny ice piece
In the land where my eyebrows and tears froze
I had no time to grieve over his death

The day I got the "akagami"
I was prepared to die on the battlefield
In the battlefield called Mudanjiang
Though I didn't fight
I was a part of the war
Then August 15, 1945
I listened to the "Gyoku-on Hoso"
The real voice of Emperor Hirohito
Japan has been defeated
But hell has just begun
As soon as we were about to return
Tall foreign soldiers captured us
I was pushed into the dark freight train
Before the heavy door closed
I saw the mark on the soldiers' uniform
Red square.
Golden hammer and sickle.
A star.

Stalin's army.
Every single day
I cut down trees
Frost bit into my barefoot like knives
Every single day
I heard objects falling in the snow
Not our footsteps
Neither the pile of snow falling from the trees
But our companions dropping dead
One. By. One
Every single day
Soup with no ingredients and coarse bread were breakfast,
lunch, and dinner
Every single day
Freezing winds blew on us
As if gods were mocking us
Every single day
All I can do
Looking up at the white sky
Hoping that in the future
Peaceful
Tranquil
Amicable days will continue
For eternity

Noah Leong, Grade 9
Lowell High School, San Francisco County
Anne Torres, Classroom Teacher
Susan Terence, Poet Teacher

Sioki, Inside My Heart

Inside my heart is my dog, Sioki
a husky as tall as a bookcase

with brown, white, and gray fur.
Sioki, as soft as my stuffed animals.

Sioki loves to play with my soccer ball
and his favorite color is blue.

Valerie Hermosillo, Grade 2
Logan Memorial Educational Campus, San Diego County
Barbara Lekes, Classroom Teacher
Johnnierenee Nelson, Poet Teacher

Childhood

I am the son of wide sidewalks, bicycle rickshaws,
stray cats and dogs,
Cars coughing exhaust fumes that smell like rotten eggs,
Sleeping mats made of split bamboo
Always going outside to play
Going back inside for lunch

Living under a roof with two stories and an attic
Ladder leads to missing pieces from the attic wall
Don't know why it's like that
Don't really care
Childlike curiosity leads to watching neighbors through walls

My older sister, Kyi Kyi Lai Lai Win,
is a sly, mischievous cat
"Come outside, look!"
Only a few seconds to wonder
Where am I supposed to look
Until I am thrust back
Pointy, greenish-yellow durians catch my fall
My behind poked by dull, brown needles
Tag with neighbors on the sidewalks
She slows down, then turns and ducks
Tagger sent flying and lands on someone
Thankfully not too hurt
Slides made with rough planks of wood
Can't slide
Then
Hurry up, "Myan myan lote!" behind me,
Then hands behind me propel me
Finally sliding, but splinters speckle my behind

When we created trouble, Mama made punishment
"Go find a stick" were the dreaded words
But the long game is playable here
Wait long enough
And her anger fades away
I am the friend of the big stray dogs
Wrestling like we were a pack
Saving food for them in a large pot
Going home
Smelling like unwashed dog
Laying on split-bamboo mats
My brother, Ko Ko Kyi So Win, can't stand the smell
Says it smells so bad
So bad he can't sleep

We always tried to catch butterflies
Colorful specks floating through the air
No nets, only hands
We tried our best with what we had
Butterflies kept flying free
I was the son of catching butterflies
Stray dogs
Friendly neighbors
Making mischief
Many spankings
Kyi-Kyi-caused injuries
Watching neighbors through thin walls
But now I am
A middle-aged-man
Thousands of miles from my childhood
Working a job
A job that only sees me
As a machine to spring more work on
Yet I am also
The father of a young girl
She has

My face
Minus the age spots
Long hair
In contrast to my bald head
A dark mole
Under the double eyelids she got from her mother
All I can do is to prepare her for the world
Complain about my job
And tell her about the good ol' days
Where all I can remember was having a lot of fun
Where all I cared about was going out to play

Emilee Chan, Grade 9
Lowell High School, San Francisco County
Karen Franklin, Classroom Teacher
Susan Terence, Poet Teacher

Dear Superman in Disguise

Yes, you, with the jet black hair and brown and green eyes.
You haven't saved the world, but you sure have saved me.
Whenever I'm with you, I'm happy and free.
We listen to music on the way back to school
and watch our favorite shows and play in the pool.
You tell me funny jokes, even if some don't make me laugh
and during my plays, you're in the front row, the first one to clap.
You take me to parks, and push me on the swing.
If I had all day to write this I would write everything
you do to make me laugh, you do to make me smile,
writing this poem didn't even take a while.
Your power to be funny, calm and carefree
is just one of the things you do to inspire me.
You make me and my brother dinner, even if I don't eat all my food
and I really hope someday, that I can repay you.
You wait for me to wake up, so we can awake our dog together.
I just want you to know I love you, and I will forever and ever.
You let me stay up late so we can watch TV and talk,
and in New York, we go get ice cream, and go on nice long walks.
You answer all my questions, and ask me ones, too.
I used to think you knew everything, but now I know you do.
You know how to make me laugh, and how to make me cry
and before I leave for school, you give me a kiss goodbye.
You may not be a hero, in someone else's eyes
but to me, you are, Superman in disguise.

Quinn Mullin, Grade 5
Strawberry Point School, Marin County
Rachel Quek, Classroom teacher
Terri Glass, Poet Teacher

Rosa Parks

Picture her, a beautiful
Tree standing tall.
Even when cut, her
Memory lives on.
Picture her as the
Wind blowing through
The mountains.
Listen to the whisper
She has left.
Picture her as the
Woman she has always
Been. Finally getting to
Shine through.
I like to think of
Her as someone
Who never gave up.
I like to think of her as
Someone who learned how
To be strong because
Of what the world put her through.

Scarlet Zhang, Grade 5
West Portal Elementary, San Francisco County
Marina DeGroot, Classroom Teacher
Susan Terence, Poet Teacher

California Poets in the Schools

A Gift to Give Away

An apple is my hand
around a sun ray,
as sweet as victory,
as lovely as a bracelet of friendship,
but, all the same, a gift to give away.

A chicken with golden feathers
needing to care,
needing to love,
needing to let someone in.

I give it the apple,
to let her take flight.
Give her a thing to care for.

Now each day, I see her
head high,
the apple tucked under her wings.

Jane Hanson, Grade 6
Mountain View Elementary, Santa Barbara County
Susana Yee, Classroom Teacher
Cie Gumucio, Poet Teacher

Christopher

I taught
my best friend
the right form
to shoot a basketball.
He taught me
to trust people.
His eyes are brown
like a beautiful tree.
He wears clothes
like a rainbow.
He shines
like the sun.

Angel Lopez Ortiz, Grade 4
Roseland Elementary, Sonoma County
Krissia Santos, Classroom Teacher
Lisa Shulman, Poet Teacher

Ode to Zach Bryan

Your songs tell a story
From your past filled with wrath
The sweetness of glory
Pain sweet pain
They are just boys of faith
Fighting overtime hours
You're my holy roller
Come as you are
You saved me
Love to scream your words
Till we burn, burn, burn
All my dawns were spent with you
On my way back from El Dorado
To east side of sorrow
It becomes fifth of May
It's truly become the best of my days
We thank you for your service

Shyra Greenberg, Grade 12
Willits High School, Mendocino County
Katrina Hall, Classroom Teacher
J.W. Churchill, Poet Teacher

Here is a Sueño

I want to give you a sueño of crystal
condors soaring
in stars.
For you, a corazón of joy
in the night.
Here is a cielo of pearl
harmonicas playing their music.
Dance with the crystal condors
soaring in the pearl white stars.
Surround yourself with a bosque
of happiness.
Taste the ruby red grapefruits.
Hear the mar flowing.
Embrace the condors of crystal.
I want to give you a sueño.
For you a crystal condor.
Here is a sueño of enlightenment.

Elpidio Sy, Grade 3,
Francis Scott Key Elementary, San Francisco County
May Chung, Classroom Teacher
Susan Terence, Poet Teacher

Gone

Gone is the wind after rain.
Gone are the tears after pain.
Gone are the leaves after a storm.
Gone are the threads after a shirt is torn.
Gone are the dreams after I awake.
Gone is my money after a toothache.
Here I am, take my hand,
hold my hand, for I am right here
by your side. I will never leave you,
I am never gone.

Zoey Gai, Grade 6
Jacoby Creek Elementary School, Humboldt County
Lauren Sanzaro, Classroom Teacher
Dan Zev Levinson, Poet Teacher

For Dad

I would give you a life
so that we can be together.

I would give you my bracelet
that we made years ago.

I would beg for a pet
to keep you company when I'm gone.

I would give you this poem to warm your heart.

Adam Krejsbol, Grade 5
Pleasant Valley Elementary, Marin County
DeMaur Herrera, Classroom Teacher
Lea Aschkenas, Poet Teacher

Ode to Our Classroom

You are filled with lots
Of books.

You help us to learn
All the things around us.

You help us
Ace math!

When we go home,
Your desks get up and fly;
The dinosaurs come alive
From the skeleton drawer.

Student Group Poem, Grade 3
Coleman Elementary, Marin County
Sasha Sanchez, Classroom Teacher
Virginia Barrett, Poet Teacher

To Tootsie Roll, My Hamster

I will give you all the blueberries you want
so we can have a contest again.
I will buy you more tubes to wiggle through
so you don't get bored.
I'll clean your cage every weekend
so it doesn't smell.
I'll play with you to see you grow.
I'll watch you get weaker every day.
And I'll watch as you pass and your body gets stiff.
And then I'll give you my lung to live another day.
And I'll even grow my garden back
for you to play in one more time.

Aster Kicherer, Grade 5
Pleasant Valley Elementary, Marin County
DeMaur Herrera, Classroom Teacher
Lea Aschkenas, Poet Teacher

Lin Manuel Miranda

You don't get enough credit for what you do
singing, dancing, writing, this is how I feel about you
you write songs and sing
each note is a bell ring
each rhyme is a beat
each word is a treat
each song is an abundance of smiles
each piece of music goes ten thousand miles
with a voice meant to rap
and a mouth meant to smile
and feet meant to tap
and hands meant to hold,
the microphone too long to be told
Hamilton gives the Broadway feel
Encanto was quite the deal
Moana is an ocean breeze
The Little Mermaid, under the seas
In the Heights that touched the skies
and many more that were not brought to mind
Nice work, a thousand times
That work made your days very full
You are the one thing in life you can control
you are an original.

P.S. I would name all your songs,
but that would take too long

Ellora Nag, Grade 5
Strawberry Point School, Marin County
Rachel Quek, Classroom Teacher
Terri Glass, Poet Teacher

Salmon Kin

I
barely remember
you, Grampa.
When I think of
you, sweets, lots of
sweets, salmon, rich tasty
salmon, and home, sweet
home. You are still with
us, as salmon kin.
We are
salmon kin.

Aviva Asantewaa, Grade 5
Mattole Elementary, Humboldt County
Nick Tedesco, Classroom Teacher
Dan Zev Levinson, Poet Teacher

I Want to Give You A...

I want to give you a sueño, a dream of
        wonders.
Water lilies are flying in the valley.
For you, a song of peace
In the clouds up above.
Here is the night of the breeze.
Peaches fly off the branches.
Dance with the light, with the birds.
The birds fly in the Big Dipper.
Surround yourself with a coat
Of love.
Taste the sky and the wetlands water.
Hear the chirping birds and the squirming
Worms.

Eloise Berkman, Grade 3
Francis Scott Key Elementary, San Francisco County
Sarah Chan, Classroom Teacher
Susan Terence, Poet Teacher

Ode to My Cat, Fefe

Your fur was the color of a cloudy thunderstorm.
Your ears were as green as jade.
Your fur was as warm as the sun.
Your purr was as long as a river.
You gave me happiness when I was sad.

Avila Greene, Grade 3
Pleasant Valley Elementary, Marin County
Sarah Dooher, Classroom Teacher
Lea Aschkenas, Poet Teacher

Give Love

I want to give you a love poem of hearts
drifting through the air.
In the ponds are swans following you gifting
presents like a box of love just for you.
Just dance with all the animals and people around
you with the sun shining down on you.
Surround yourself with love and happiness all
around you.
All of the families around you are clapping and
cheering for you and you feel loved and safe.
It is like you can taste all the love and happiness on
your tongue almost like you can hear the animals
whispering, "good job and we love you,"
and you just feel like this is the best day ever.

Nora Loveday-Smith, Grade 3
Francis Scott Key Elementary, San Francisco County
Katherine Johnson, Classroom Teacher
Susan Terence, Poet Teacher

What Books Never Taught

I watched the town I grew up in blow into pieces of bricks, wood
And pieces of flesh from the ones whom I met before
who never will reappear again.
I couldn't help but fly away like a bird hopelessly.
I was young and had no choice.
Years have passed and I've returned to my homeland
Hoping to see familiar faces and homes
But see nothing but death, cries, and rubbish.
I watched the lizi and longan tree remain
nothing but a burnt stump.
There were nothing but crisps of wood
and ashes in my hometown.
I cried and I cried and I cried but
there was no choice left but to restart again.
I went to school and read books
that taught me how beautiful the world is,
How people smiled and shared flowers with love and care
But not about the cruelty behind it
Never about the greed of people and the ugly beasts inside them.
How I wish none of this would have happened
And never left me with my home as rubbish
But there is no more time for tears to run through my eyes again.
I'll stand up like one hundred, one thousand,
one million others to repair
And rebuild our homeland that has been destroyed by war.
I will no longer hide but to stand up high to protect our home.

Yongyi Chen, Grade 9
Lowell High School, San Francisco County
Bryan Ritter, Classroom Teacher
Susan Terence, Poet Teacher

Misha

(my great grandpa)

I am a survivor.
When I was six years old WWII entered my childhood.

I was with my grandparents when the war started.
I remember my grandfather
opening the barn and letting all the animals out.

I remember his face...
it changed in front of me in a single day.
I remember my grandmother
telling us all to come into the house.

I am standing in front of a train with so many other people
How did I get here?

Why is there so much smoke in the air?
We get on the train and I hear a horrible noise

I am thrown against a wall,
then another, whose arm is this?
The train is being bombed.

I remember being cut with glass and
being thrown onto the punishing grass.
My entire body is a mess and aching,
but I get up and run towards the thick trees.

Please help me!

The Ukrainian woods were my home for the next week.
The things I saw on that deafening afternoon
on the train will stay with me forever...

The screams, the dead, where is mama?

I learn to pick cotton, but sadly it does not like me.
After evacuating to Uzbekistan,
I work with my family on the cotton field.

After two days, my eyes shut down and I can no longer see.
Did I go blind, why?

A week in total darkness lifted,
and I never returned to the field to pick cotton, why did it take
my sight?
I hear the adults tell stories at night,
so many family members are dead or missing,
I keep looking at the sky wondering
about bombs flying around like a comet on a starry night.

Although I don't see them now, it doesn't mean they won't return.

Days pass, I am always hungry, will I ever get to eat.
I hear from a man, "the war is over!"

What does it mean?
I am yet to ever go to school.

I am ten, but I don't know how to read.
I hear my aunt say, "they will teach him".

I start school, not sure why my papers say I am eight years old,
Did they make a mistake?

Slowly the letters begin to come together and finally I see words.
My aunt was right.

I am 11 and hunger is not what occupies my head anymore.
I am Misha, and I am here to stay.

Mia Pinski, Grade 9
Lowell High School, San Francisco County
Torie Palmer, Classroom Teacher
Susan Terence, Poet Teacher

The Journey

My people come from the faraway lands of Vietnam
The boat
Broken
Wet
Shades of brown and black
Worn out
Thorns and wood sticking out like thumbtacks
The engine of the boat running on the water
The rusty engine holding on for dear life
Smells of fish
Scents of smoke
Atmosphere filled with sweat
The aroma of my people

My people
Taller than me
Bigger than me
Strong than me
Crowded like a group of ants around sugar
Barely holding together
Random but familiar
My parents beside me
Their calloused but soft hands on my shoulder
Like a lychee
Cool like the wind
Comforting like a blanket
They look straight at me
Nothing said
Nothing needed

My sister behind them
Shorter than me
Younger than me
Her eyes concentrated on me
Like a hawk on a mouse
Her eyes were still as soft as a pillow
Giving me warmth
Without them, I had nothing
Together I had everything
Without them, the journey would be endless
Together it felt like a second

Jason Trieu, Grade 9
Lowell High School, San Francisco County
Jesse Hannawalt, Classroom Teacher
Susan Terence, Poet Teacher

El Atardecer

Y el cielo vuelve a llover
Una gota que acaricia el mar
Aunque ya nada sea como ayer
No pienses que ya te olvidé

Aquel sueño del que desperté
Me hace llorar por que tú
ya no estas y aunque no eres para mí
No pienses que ya te olvidé

Me siento vacía sin ti
Yo ya no sé lo que es sonreir

Nos miramos bajo el atardecer
Tú tan elegante como te recordé
y aunque ya no estés
No pienses que ya te olvidé

The Sunset

And the sky rains again
A drop that caresses the sea
Although nothing is like yesterday
Don't think that I've already forgotten you

That dream from which I woke up
Makes me cry because you are no longer there
And although you are not for me
Don't think that I've already forgotten you

I feel empty without you
I no longer know what it is to smile

We look at each other under the sunset
You as elegant as I remembered
And although you are no longer here
Don't think that I've forgotten you

Noemi Garcia, Grade 11
Willits High School, Mendocino County
Katrina Hall, Classroom Teacher
J.W. Churchill, Poet Teacher

The Peach Tree at 1641

Did you eat yet?
you always made sure I ate
coming home from school you always made me a plate:
taken from the backyard,
a peach laid on the lawn
it was the fruit of your labor that made me live on
how you cut the peach, brought the sweetness of my youth
and the blossoms bloomed a pink delicate hue
it was in July that made the peach tree shine
in the summer breeze it was all mine
Did you eat yet?
not asking me but the tree:
in September I remember,
you fed the peach tree sugar to sweeten the taste
because you said that the ripest of fruits are grown from the roots
and you cannot stand bitter fruits:
from here to Cagayan,
that is where your roots belong
from then to now,
your memories are yet to go along:
with you the day was new
and from old wounds you bloomed
reminding me of your past with memories of the passed
you were born from fruitless trees, they wilted from hunger,
and this is why you made sure I ate
Did you eat yet, Anak?
he said in his Ilocano accent, so strong and near:
just as my grandfather the tree fed me fruit
just as my lolo the memories start to take root:
as the seasons change my tree is displaced,
the vivid leaves have wilted to waste
now in December he has changed with the weather

with the tree, he has changed altogether
Did you eat yet?
asking me one last time
the last bite of his labor was now sour and bitter
the tree had died with him in December
sitting out my window, I look outside;
the once nourished branches
are now where his memories will resign
with every glance I take I hope to see him tending to the tree,
because I am forever in need
now I ask myself, where do my roots belong at 1641?

Juniper Carrasco, Grade 11
Channel Islands High School, Ventura County
Kimberly Tahsuda, Classroom Teacher
Fernando Salinas, Poet Teacher

My Family

My Mother is the most wonderful woman in the world
My Mother takes care of me and makes me soup when I'm sick
She doesn't pick me up when I fall down
she teaches me how to get back up again
My Mother has been taking care of me and
teaching me lessons ever since I was born

My Father is the best Dad in the world
He is really funny and strong
He helps me to learn volleyball
He buys me the material I need for my school and sports
He supports me with my decisions
Like what sport I like or what I love to do
My Father is the best father in the world

I am the only child in my family
I ask for things but I'm grateful for them
I might be an only child but I might not get what I want
but I'm happy for what I have
I love my family

Kayla Hernandez, Grade 6
Nicasio School, Marin County
Kristy Snaith, Classroom Teacher
Michele Rivers, Poet Teacher

Tita Likes to Say

I don't ever remember a time without Tita.
She might even have taught me my very first word,
Gatas which means milk in Tagalog.

As a baby, she held me tight in her arms.
As a toddler, she made me giggle
and loved to see me dance into the New Year
when at the stroke of midnight
she threw handfuls of two-dollar bills into the air
to catch for good luck.

Tita is fun and full of laughter.
Tita loves to cook and host parties.
"Eat! Eat! Eat!" she insists — "Sige, na. Kain na!" —
as she fills your paper plate with a heap of steaming rice.
At the parties I learned that it was polite to go for seconds
to show Tita how much you love her food.

But also at these parties, Tita likes to say, "Tumataba ka na."
"Taba," means fat in Tagalog.
Therefore, Tita likes to say, "You're getting fat,"
Before and after all that food.

She says it ALWAYS.
Honestly, I hear it said all the time.
In all the parties, in all directions.
Almost like a greeting,
A rude "Hello."

No one is spared.
Pinsan my Cousin isn't spared.
Tito my Uncle isn't spared.
Kuya or *Ate* isn't spared.
Lolo or *Lola* isn't spared.
I am not spared.

The sad thing is, Tita doesn't spare even herself.

Lola says that it is just part of "the culture."
Tito says it's just a joke because she says it with a laugh.
And they all swear that it is harmless.
But none of that is true for me.

Helena Donato-Sapp, Grade 10
Orange County School of the Arts, Los Angeles County
Nancy Woo, Poet Teacher

My Family

I appreciate that my mom pushes me to do better
I love my mom's delicious tacos
My mom works as hard as a bee
Caretaker, she is a hero

I appreciate my dad he works hard at a dairy ranch
I like watching soccer games with my dad,
we cheer for Chivas teams
It's just me and Dad on the couch,
not any of my sisters, which is my favorite

I am the funny one in my family,
I bug my sisters, but not every day though
I'm the comedian and I love my family a lot
I can't imagine being without them

Jaciel Diaz, Sixth Grade
Nicasio School, Marin County
Kristy Snaith, Classroom Teacher
Michele Rivers, Poet Teacher

My Grandpa

My grandpa who is from China
Who calls me Jo
Who tells me to focus on Mandarin
Who remembers his home in Shanghai
Whose eyes are a soft cloudy desert
Whose hands are soft on my skin and
sharp while cooking
Who feeds me joy in the afternoon
Whose voice is like soft cotton
touching my heart
He is a piano playing with the ocean

Johanna Ngo, Grade 3
Francis Scott Key Elementary, San Francisco County
Sarah Chan, Classroom Teacher
Susan Terence, Poet Teacher

My Loving Parents

Inside my heart
are my mom and dad.

They love me and
they take me to the park.

They play with me
after they have taken care of me.

They take me to school
and to Chollas Lake
to feed the ducks.

They feed me lasagna!

Noelani Yom, Grade 2
Logan Memorial Educational Campus, San Diego County
Barbara Lekes, Classroom Teacher
Johnnierenee Nelson, Poet Teacher

My Friends

I learned from
my friends to
be a kind
friend back

They say Hola and
make my day
it makes me
happy like butterflies

We would hold
hands and skip
like bunnies around
the field

We wore green
shirts for green
eggs and ham
we looked funny

In their eyes
I see kindness
shining bright

With them I
know how to
be brave

Aaliyah Vega Valenzuela, Grade 4
Roseland Elementary, Sonoma County
Steve Ciaffa, Classroom Teacher
Lisa Shulman, Poet Teacher

I'll Give You

I'll give you a letter to remind you of the fun we had.
I'll give you a smooth stone for you to grasp when you feel alone.
I'll give you lightning in a bottle for you to hold your anger in.
I'll give you a passion fruit that can remind you
when you bite into it that you can be bitter and
sweet just like the fruit.
I'll give you a shell from the bottom of the ocean
so when you put your ear to it you'll find the
sound of crashing waves.
I'll give you a prayer for you to keep close to your heart.
I'll give you a pencil so you can write back.

Evelyn Cox, Grade 4
Mountain View Elementary, Santa Barbara County
Katherine James, Classroom Teacher
Cie Gumucio, Poet Teacher

Last Summer

Last Summer I flew on the airplane
Only Me,
barely seven years old
and Owen,
my 5 year old cousin.
We were going to visit my Aunt Maria
aka Owen's Mimi,
And her all grown up son, McKeever.
I hoped McKeever would teach me to drive
down Maria's long private road
that twists like a snake in tall grass.
Maria lives in the land of open fields,
cool green grass,
no people around for miles and miles
Owen and I come from the Bay Area
with Neighbors all around us
clogged freeways,
and strip malls by the mile.
I love summers in Eugene best.
You can play with nerf guns
inside the house
float down a river in inner tubes
jump as high as Michael Jordan
at the trampoline park
eat slushies made from mangos
eat McDonalds in the city park
and ride dirt bikes every morning.
My family is made of movies
about fast and fancy cars.
My ancestors love it
when I laugh out loud.
My roots are made of

Golden State Warriors Championships
Bob Dylan Songs
and dancing in the kitchen
at home with my little brother
and my dog, Angel.

Sydney Cirelli, Grade 3
Malcolm X Elementary, Alameda County
Suzanne Middleton Fraser, Classroom Teacher
Milani Pelley, Poet Teacher

I Will Send You

I will send you a paper airplane so you can go anywhere
whenever you want.

I will send you the color green so you can feel like nature is right
by your side.

I will send you a camel so you can travel through the Sahara
Desert.

I will send you a telescope so you can see all the beautiful
stars.

I will send you a call so it feels like we're together again.

Lucas Friedman, Grade 4
Montecito Union School, Santa Barbara County
Shannon Gallup, Classroom Teacher
Cie Gumucio, Poet Teacher

Gifts

I want to give you a dream of yellow eagles
flying in the clouds
For you a ring of happiness in the summer
Here's a bosque (forest) of green pinecones
dropping down and rolling
away
Dance with the diamond bear
Run in the sun
Surround yourself in a river of trees
Taste the future
Hear the moon welcoming you

Asa Alexander, Grade 3
Francis Scott Key Elementary, San Francisco County
May Chung, Classroom Teacher
Susan Terence, Poet Teacher

You

I am offering this poem to the hospital
I visited you in
the place you left
and everything changed.
You give me thoughts of what we would do,
how we could have been so close,
had things in common
thoughts of hanging out
thoughts of how everything would be different.
Today I put the gifts of you on an altar made of words
purple butterflies flying for you
your song playing for you
cattails will be growing for you.
This offering is strong like the wind.
Reminding me of the first time I ever met you
You are a change
a difference
an impact
You help me understand that time is short
that I must make the most of everyone and everything
Guiding me through patience, thought and sacrifice
Thank you for your time
You make me a better me

Zurielle Herrera, Grade 7
Manchester School, Mendocino County
Avis Anderson, Classroom Teacher
Blake More, Poet Teacher

My California

My Bolinas

In my Bolinas, waves crash on sandy rocks
while noisy gulls screech overhead
The rain pounds on the roof of my cottage
while hummingbirds bathe on the fence
In my Bolinas, wind rushes fog over Mt. Tam
to the Golden Gate
The redwoods reflect over the estuary in the moonlight,
as the sun sets over the far away horizon
They mirror my name
In my Bolinas, the lone coyote waits by the road
and I think of Tia barking
In my Bolinas, sand crabs burrow by the groin
and tiger sharks swish
among empty clam shells
My paddle board glides by the old swing
in the back muddy canals of the Estuary
The mossy fallen tree blocks the entrance
like a hidden underwater gate
On the banks, bush leaves are completely covered
by many layers of cormorant, pelican, and egret droppings
They reek of fish
In my Bolinas, the dock hides ocean treasures
while we humans enjoy
coffee, pastries, and burritos from the Coast Cafe
My Bolinas is perfect

Oceanna Stewart, Grade 6
Mill Valley Middle School, Marin County
Brenda Poletti, Classroom Teacher
Claire Blotter, Poet Teacher

Blue California

(a mash-up poem)

Blue is like the crashing car
that is fun like a basketball player.
Blue looks like a blue whale
that just made a blue splash in
the ocean that is blue.
I would eat a blue blueberry instead
of a football that is hard as a rock.
I am able to get mad easily
like the kind robot going insane.
Blue sounds like a person
that has blue skin and blue hair and they
squeeze basketballs out of their ears and noses.
My California
is not perfect at all.
I have changes that I would like to suggest.
#1 is to Rollerland—
The floor can be better
because there are chips in the floor
so we can fall.
I have fallen before.
The blue flowers bloom in the nature temperature.

Jewlz Domen, Grade 3
Chenoweth Elementary, Merced County
Meuy Saeteurn, Classroom Teacher
Dawn Trook, Poet Teacher

My California

Barefoot running along the narrow winding
Bridgeport trail
well-worn from the long summer
Around every corner a new surprise
A new reason to pause, observe, take it all in
Yet never long enough for my family to catch up.

Waves of California poppies, lupines, Indian
paintbrush, irises, yarrow
Stretching across both sides.

Sunset orange fairy wings hold onto the stem of
the California poppy
The name of my childhood best friend.

"The lupine lady" existing outside the book I
read almost every night
Drifting into the beautiful rolling Sierra foothills,
    purple being
        the only thing seen.

The contrast between the lush early summer green grass
soon to turn brown as if a disease spreads
and the vibrant orange of the Indian paintbrush
Always my favorite.

All being kept away in a glass box to observe
not to break or to harm but to protect
whenever shoes get kicked off, letting go, in the
company of the rainbow wildflowers
always there to shower us with beauty.

All loved enough to learn their name
All loved enough to memorize

Aislinn Welch, Grade 11
Sierra Academy of Expeditionary Learning, Nevada County
Marika Beck, Classroom Teacher
Kirsten Casey, Poet Teacher

A Day Like Any Other in My California

Sticky, amber sap, dripping lazily
in the sweltering late afternoon sun
The river has at last calmed
glowing emerald algae.
Slide over the slippery, slanting granite
like a northern water snake
leap heedlessly from boulder to boulder
over deep, swirling pools.
And when the balls of your feet begin to burn
on the ember rocks
tentatively dip them in the snow melt water.
Let them soften like your sun-bleached curls
swimsuit dripping on the steaming tar in the parking lot.
We'll walk through town after
wrapped in our sarongs
sandals squeaking
chests and shoulders red as the
tiny strawberries we'll buy from the farmer's market
Then we'll turn our weary eyes to the horizon
and watch in silent awe as, just for a moment,
the sun's last rays reach out
and submerge the world in gold.

Emma McBurney, Grade 11
Sierra Academy of Expeditionary Learning, Nevada County
Marika Beck, Classroom Teacher
Kirsten Casey, Poet Teacher

A Tale of Two Cities

For some it's the best of times
For others it's the worst of times

Home prices rising on the east end
Tents dropping along the streets
Homeless laying by the curbside
Their outcome not made intentionally
Most folks ignore–
They are indifferent, they are elite

Driving in their pampering SUV's
Passing shopping carts filled with people's dreams
Reading "help me" signs from poor esteems
Glad they got their four-year degrees

Living in the suburbs is a cushy life
Kept from the people through redline
Million-dollar homes and the marginalized
Some take it easy, some work to survive

Cost of living increasing with time
Some work two jobs, some resort to crime.
Six-figure salaries are in short supply...
Is the Golden State starting to lose its shine?

Surrounded by wealth, yet many left behind
For some luxury only exists behind the Hollywood sign
A population excluded by design
For once they must be prioritized

And yet,
A new generation is emerging
Maybe they will bring the change that we are yearning
As a collective it is time to decide
Now is the time of Do or Die.
Now is the time to make things Right.
Now is the time for us to Unite.

Sofia Uribe, Grade 11
Millikan High School, Los Angeles County
Nancy Woo, Poet Teacher

My California

The deep blue dress that I wore as a kid
The color reflecting the river where I spent my days
Small feet buried in hot sand
Absorbing sun greedily without care
for how much is left for others
Run Jump Splash
Sand unsticking from my arms and legs and
falling to the bottom
Clean body
Pure soul
Except for the grains of sand I will find later
under my fingernails on the car ride home
The water holds me with care
Head tilted back and eyes squinting closed
Water lapping against my head and ears
The gentle sound and current pushing against me
Providing a comfort only the river and my mom can provide
Plunging my head under the water surrounding me
cold but needed against the heat of the sun
I open my eyes in the clear water and watch
as the small pike minnow swims by
Making eye contact with him
Trying to explain I mean him no harm
My breath held tight and my feet kicking
to the algae-covered rock bottom
My legs and feet turning into a tail
Green and shimmering
Flowing through the water and pushing me faster
Until I come up for air and turn
back to human

Soleil Ophira Johnson, Grade 11
Sierra Academy of Expeditionary Learning, Nevada County
Marika Beck, Classroom Teacher
Kirsten Casey, Poet Teacher

California Poets in the Schools

The World as We Know It

Foaming, glistening, hues of green and blue
winding down the mountain top
In my California, the saltless waters don't sting
like hornets on bitten tongues,
they taste of earth, taste of home
Algae swirls like vacant spirits cast to the depths
Pine trees tower like giants,
golden shields raised to the rest of the world
Protecting us from its harshness
Concrete blankets these once abundant meadows
Laying to rest in permanent slumber
In my California, we rest our backs on pavement,
looking to the immeasurable
expanse of our polluted skies
Still, boundless stars stab through the tainted atmosphere
and illuminate the night
In my California, the woods light ablaze,
shifting in the center of us
A delicate breeze could be injurious
Embers glide with such impressive elegance,
a thousand shimmering fireflies
Orange like a sea of countless tiny poppies
In my California, the sun streaks across the sky
An oil painting, each stroke determining our futures here
Wish you were somewhere else?
In my California, we dance with the inevitable passage of time
As the years flow by, like a river
Ceaselessly passing through us
Try and grab onto a rock if you can
Before the rapids tear you up

Bella O'Dale, Grade 11
Sierra Academy of Expeditionary Learning, Nevada County
Marika Beck, Classroom Teacher
Kirsten Casey, Poet Teacher

Hollywood Sign

I remember Hollywood, and seeing the Hollywood sign,
With big white letters,
With so much meaning to their city.
Hollywood has stars
On the floor
For actors, and others.

You can pay
To get your name
On a star.

Mia Flores, Grade 8
San Fernando Middle School, Los Angeles County
David Malley, Classroom Teacher
Juan Cardenas, Poet Teacher

Summers at the Land

The sun rises over the purple mountains
Casting the forest in color, bright, alive, awake
The cool night air still lingers,
fighting against the encroaching heat
The Northern California summer slowly rising,
basking our yurt in golden light

A ring of sunshine drops through the skylight
Settling into place, a circle on the carpet
where the colors have bleached,
Light yellow, faint red, a whisper of blue

We drag our bikes up the hill to the gate,
Dried brown pine needles crunch beneath our feet
Ring the bell and we're off
Zooming down the hill at full speed,
Turn around and race back up
Over and over and over again

Faces flushed, we stand knee deep in the lazy creek,
the cold water numbing our toes, mosquitos buzzing hungrily
Fingers stained purple
Blackberry juice running down our chins
Dunk your face in the water, a cold shock to the system
A taste of winter snow, melted high in the Sierras

The dusk wanders in lazily
The sun lingers like a child at bedtime
The campfire crackles, marshmallows falling into the ashes

The sun sinks down behind the purple mountains
Even in July, they still wear their white caps of snow

Mariposa Freeling, Grade 11
Sierra Academy of Expeditionary Learning, Nevada County
Marika Beck, Classroom Teacher
Kirsten Casey, Poet Teacher

Who I Am,
Where I Come From

It's Sacred

Song And Dance
To Some Means Nothing
But To Us It's Sacred

Michael Williams, Grade 12
South Valley High School, Mendocino County
Kirsten Tuner, Classroom Teacher
J.W. Churchill, Poet Teacher

No One Knows...

I am the smooth jet owl flying in the wind,
but I wish I was the fresh diamond coral
glowing in the clouds.
No one knows I am really a quiet rust wand,
soaring in the sky.
Everybody thinks I am perfect, but I am not.
Every day, I want to hide in my shell
away from everybody
because they keep asking me questions
and I just want to go to my bed and fall asleep.
I come home tired from flying and soaring in the sky
and go to bed.
I know tomorrow will be a new day.

Jayden Wei, Grade 3
Francis Scott Key Elementary, San Francisco County
May Chung, Classroom Teacher
Susan Terence, Poet Teacher

Untitled

My eyes are a crystal puffy sadness.
My hair is like a smooth soft wavy ocean.
My hands are a rough topaz.
My spirit is a sad silky sapphire.
I become a strike of lightning when I'm mad.
I dream of the sun and moon.
I wish for happiness.
I miss my old self.
Sometimes I feel like I would be sad forever.

Marcus Adam Vergara, Grade 4
Longfellow Elementary, San Francisco County
Victoria Lanterman, Classroom Teacher
Susan Terence, Poet Teacher

Where I'm From

I am from the West Portal
From courage the cowardly dog and Victoria's Secret
I am from the yellow daisy
Aged, Victorian
It felt comforting
I am from the moss, the dandelion
Yellow flower to light air
I'm from the road trips and rodeos
From Naya and Kyrin and Brenda
I'm from the unspoken communication and laughter
From "treat others the way you want to be treated"
And "it's your actions not your words"
I'm from different spiritualities
From crystals to Christianity
I'm from San Marcos, BBQ and pop
From the time we were on a road trip
And my brother got his foot stuck in a trap
The football addict mom
To the pictures in the living room
I am Natalynn and I'm from Texas
And I'm just a curious person

Natalynn Cockrum, Grade 11
Big Picture Ukiah at South Valley High School, Mendocino County
Kirsten Turner, Classroom Teacher
J.W. Churchill, Poet Teacher

A Journey of Music

I am winter; cold, cloudy, and gloomy.
I am where my dad came from; Juarez, Zacatecas, Mexico.
Where the parade of the "Sagrado Corazon de Jesus"
happens every year in June;
With loud music and bright colors.
This tradition is 72 years old.

I am the music I listen to.
When I listen to R&B, I think about my mom
and how she would play it on the radio
And talk about how she would listen to it
when she was younger.
When I hear Mexican music like Norteña and Cumbias,
I think of my dad and how he would
listen to it when he works,
And how he dances to it.

When I listen to Bachata,
I think about how the rhythm sounds
And how expressive it could be.

I am from a country that had indigenous people and tribes.
I have seen an indigenous man with earrings,
And he looks a bit old.
He goes out and to take pictures of eagles in the sky,
And he would paint them, or sketch them with a pencil.

Jazmine Rodriguez, Grade 7
San Fernando Middle School, Los Angeles County
David Malley, Classroom Teacher
Juan Cardenas, Poet Teacher

I Am a Girl

I am Sophia; Celeste Mendoza Perez;
The daughter of two High School Kids in love,
A niña who is still small and unsure on what she wants in life,
Seen as a baby who needs help with everything,
A girl who uses songs for help,
The silly cousin who rarely goes to Mexico,
The last child of a family of 5,
Just a girl who loves her family, her life and everything,
A child just a child who wants to be the type of pretty
everyone wants to be,
The girl who is described as little and small,
A girl who will turn into a caring mom,
Una niña que le molesta todo,
Who tries to love every part of her life.
I am just a girl named Sophia. Celeste Mendoza Perez.

Sophie Mendoza, Grade 7
San Fernando Middle School, Los Angeles County
David Malley, Classroom Teacher
Juan Cardenas, Poet Teacher

Maruchan Connections

My favorite food is Maruchan. A mi me gusta el Maruchan porque está muy rico y porque me gusta desde que era pequeña. When I eat Maruchan, I remember eating it for the first time with my sisters when I was little. I also remember eating it with my best friends, like almost every day.

Yo pienso que cuando primero probe Maruchan fue cuando tenia 6 años porque mis hermanas me hicieron probarlo. When I try Maruchan I remember how Mexico looks and how it is there. It also reminds me of my friends and sisters. I love how Maruchan tastes, and I love the sweet smell of it. Lime shrimp Maruchan is the best, since it's the first Maruchan flavor I ever tried. It tastes so good.

Kenia Buenrrostro, Grade 7
San Fernando Middle School, Los Angeles County
David Malley, Classroom Teacher
Juan Cardenas, Poet Teacher

Bauhinia

I came from tropical, muggy, dense air
Humid summers and streets so compact and crowded,
you stumble as people push and
shove
Cars honk coming down narrow alleyways
Of bright red signs and banners
Hanging from tall buildings
With cracked, fading paint
Street vendors yelling
In a disappearing language
Every mutter and breath
Its teachings fade and no longer passed down
Sweet, fluffy, golden bo lo baos with a soft crunchy topping
that melts on your tongue
The sugary bread breathes a scent
Forming long lines
just for a taste

I came from nothing
Of "men only" schooling and child labor
Red, blistering fingers
On small, smooth, 10-year-old hands
Blood and sweat sewn through fibers
Threads through rough sheets of silk and cotton
Paid in pennies, not even enough
For a small bowl of rice
Once penniless
Now a towering stock building
Bathing my lineage
In wealth and luxury
Living like royalty
In the fairytale of our dreams

I came from a colony
Red, blue, and white
A close sister
To the home of freedom and liberty
Bounded to a contract
That had been keeping the tropical city
safe and hidden
Covered by the warmth of our last remains
of democracy and wealth
The chains soon break and shatter
They'll envelope us, force us to loyalty
They'll reap our benefits
And leave us equal with nothing
And so like many, we drain our life savings
For a boat, a plane,
A visa
Across the Pacific
To the land of opportunity
We'd rather live with nothing but freedom
Then everything but liberty

Kaylee Luk, Grade 9
Lowell High School, San Francisco County
Bryan Ritter, Classroom Teacher
Susan Terence, Poet Teacher

What I Can and Can't Do with My Hands

My hands can help animals
because they keep getting attacked
because people think that they are a threat.

My hands can stop people
from judging LGBTQ+ people.
My hands can help Israel and Palestine.
My hands can help prevent wildfires and
stop world hunger.

My hands can't go back
to the past, can't rewind time.
My hands can't pick up a tree.

Mariska Durazo, Grade 3
Logan Memorial Educational Campus, San Diego County
Lindsay Thompson, Classroom Teacher
Johnnierenee Nelson, Poet Teacher

Big Bird

The shows in Las Vegas,
The best paintings; and
People in the club.
I am my Mom's Pozole,
Caldo de Pollo with arroz and Mole;
the spicy one.
I am Mexican culture,
The music from King Sol,
All flavors in the food.

David Becerril Jimenez, Grade 7
San Fernando Middle School, Los Angeles County
David Malley, Classroom Teacher
Juan Cardenas, Poet Teacher

The Sacred

There's a shade of blue somewhere between
Niagara Falls and puddle
It's the color of the tiles in my kitchen
And the walls of the old bathroom
My older sister's favorite color is blue
I painted her a dolphin and gave it to her for her birthday

Home Depot offers free color samples,
and I have one called brushed aluminum
It's the color of the concrete in my backyard
And the redone patch of road down the street
I bought chalk with my neighbor and we
made a four square court there

My younger sister had a bowl cut in first grade
And her bangs never quite grew back
One time we crashed a wedding to retrieve her soccer ball

When I used to finger paint,
I made masterpieces that became Christmas ornaments on the tree
The paint dried and stained my hands green
My fingers looked like feathers and I thought I could fly

Thursday nights are for butternut squash ravioli,
sausages, and peas
Wednesday nights are for chili and cornbread,
or lasagna at my grandma's house
I broke the rice cooker on accident
and we haven't gotten a new one yet

A rush of blood to the head creates bright yellow stars
I found this out when I was doing handstands
with my brother on the lawn
We tried to catch the falling stars and put them in our pockets
but we were always left empty-handed

California Poets in the Schools

One minute, we're dancing in pink tutus
across the makeshift stage of our house
The next, we're on a plane to New York,
six tickets there and five tickets back
And after that my dog will stop sitting on my bed
because it will just be an empty mattress
And then my parents won't have to remind anyone
to get their socks from the laundry area or clean off
the counters
And that is when the hunger of a young wolf is gone

Mira Sridharan, Grade 10
The Branson School, Marin County
Neha Kamdar, Classroom Teacher
Maxine Flasher-Düzgüneş, Poet Teacher

Mornings in Mexico

I am the pueblo, the air, the early Sundays in my dad's arms,
Le panadero, the ice cream man.
The early Monday mornings,
Me jumping the fence,
My neighborhood friends,
Getting chased by the cows,
Me taking a taxi to Guadalajara to either visit my uncle
In el bote, or just to go for a fun day.
Late nights when I would stay up
Waiting to see the sunrise.

Kimberly Hernandez, Grade 7
San Fernando Middle School, Los Angeles County
David Malley, Classroom Teacher
Juan Cardenas, Poet Teacher

Family Roots

lady liberty once called to my parents with praise
so that they would abandon their roots
and adjust to strange foreign ways
they faced discrimination
lack of education
yet they built a strong foundation
something that would not deter with time
because a tree without roots is nonexistent

My branches twist and wind struggling to grow
in the right direction
yearning to join those whom I share blood with
this is supposed to be me
but instead it feels as if
I'm being swallowed by the ground
in more than one occasion

the incandescent light
visible enough to be seen
everyone claps, dances, laughs
their feet moving in unison to a song I should know
the rhythm is in my veins,
I can feel it
but instead I remain seated and watch from afar

I can't relate to them
but I want to
this is supposed to be me
my branches unwinding and disconnecting

when do I grow?

I try to blend in, maybe someday
but that is not the case today
the colors of my leaves I did not choose
yet they give me away

what is so different about me, I wonder?

a silent whisper from inside escapes
"being Mexican is more than blood"
I embarked on this journey
to regain my inheritance
and when the time came for me to rise to the occasion
I had no choice but to embrace this expectation

I journeyed far and wide
to recover these fallen leaves
I followed the traces
yearned to learn about the history flowing in my veins
a known unknown mystery

the language, the flavors, the music
all native to me
but yet so unfamiliar
my roots struggled to expand
and my leaves I could not regain

where do I belong?

they say it's here
all these tias and primos I've never seen
but they ensure me this is my family
this is my culture
and I must embrace it

maybe the foundation was not as strong after all?

no I have it all wrong,
I will remember that my roots are my family
through them I feel a sense of belonging

my family born and raised in Mexico
me being the first born in this country
they see me
we may not be in the grand scheme of things
but through each other we see our belonging
after all, growing is a process
and it's the process that makes it rewarding

I recall our traditions
making tamales for Christmas
"don't add too much chicken"
cutting up vegetables for the caldo de pollo
only a few of us will eat

remembering this
I will prosper and grow
it takes more than one tree to build a forest
my own roots may not hold me down
but my father's and mother's will

Kimberli Oregel, Grade 11
Oxnard High, Ventura County
Molly Fitch, Classroom Teacher
Fernando Salinas, Poet Teacher

Plants, What I Used to Be

I used to be small,
Not just in the literal sense
I used to be quiet
Blending into the shade
Not expecting or wanting to talk at all
I used to be a lily, a baby's breath even, fragile
Tiny, just a little girl.
I miss her,
The kid I used to be...
That innocence is gone.
Now, I am a gentle giant
Someone afraid of hurting others.
A giant with a golden heart.
I'm still quiet
Still wanting to be left alone.
I'm a Redwood, standing tall
I'm an Ancient Oak, appreciating simplicity
I am brash, sarcastic, calm, neutral
I wear the same face every day
I'm worried about the state of this world.
But, I'm still me, in a vast, terrible, and beautiful universe.
I used to be small,
And now,
I am small, but full of love.

Brianna J. Clayton, Grade 8
Manchester School, Mendocino County
Avis Anderson, Classroom Teacher
Blake More, Poet Teacher

I am / Yo Soy

I am the sound of the sea that is silent and calm.
Soy el sonido en el mar que está silencioso y en calma.
I am very strong like that flower that never withers,
in the dark forest and on top of a mountain.
Soy muy fuerte como esa flor que nunca se marchita,
en el bosque oscuro y en la cima de una montaña.

I am the blue sky that is full of life and I will
always give you peace.
Soy el cielo azul que está lleno de vida y lo haré
darte siempre la paz.

I am the sand that sinks with your steps when you walk
on the beach.
Soy la arena que se hunde con tus pasos cuando caminas
en la playa.
I am the daisy that gives you happiness.
Soy la margarita que te da felicidad.

I am the tree that illuminates your loneliness.
I am the water that shines in the evening.
Soy el árbol que ilumina tu soledad.
Soy el agua que brilla en la tarde.

I am the sound, I am the flower, I am the blue sky,
I am sand, I am a daisy,
I am the tree and I am the water.
Soy el sonido, soy la flor, soy el cielo azul,
soy arena, soy una margarita,
soy el árbol y soy el agua.

Camille Buendia Mescua, Grade 7
Santa Barbara Junior High, Santa Barbara County
Patty Jo Carmean, Classroom Teacher
Cie Gumucio, Poet Teacher

Regalia Rhythm

My heart beats to the sound of regalia
clacking together at a ceremony.
Within my heart is my mom's fry bread.
My heart holds onto my first dance.
My heart is made of Yurok, Tolowa, and Karuk.
My heart craves the food after a ceremony.
Inside my heart is the pain of
having my hair done at the dance.
My heart says *chuue'* to old memories.
My heart is craving the relief after
taking off heavy regalia.
My heart holds the memory of my mom
smiling at me during my dance.

Lily Herndon, Grade 7
Blue Lake Elementary School, Humboldt County
Michelle Gibbons, Classroom Teacher
Dan Zev Levinson, Poet Teacher

I AM ME

I am a calm ocean under the night stars.
I am a wildfire spreading flames of joy everywhere.
I am an animal running free across a meadow.
I am a flower blooming full of strength.
I am a warrior fighting for peace.
I am a heart full of love.
I AM ME!!!

Avery Boyajian, Grade 3
Chenoweth Elementary, Merced County
Amy Brown, Classroom Teacher
Dawn Trook, Poet Teacher

How to Never Stop Hating Yourself (a Guide)

Start your life owing your mom's actions a purpose.
You can never forget the women that persevered, us.
Begin to notice you're "different" from the rest
You will never be a perfect American child.
You are obsessed!
Compare yourself to those born with something
you will never have.
Beautiful ocean eyes with pale white skin
in contrast to your dirty skin.
The wolf in sheep's clothing is all you will ever be.
Maybe the politicians can finally agree with someone like me.
Over analyze every single word you hear.
You are the true fear.
Remind yourself that you were looked down upon
the second you arrived.
You will never receive the sense of belonging you were deprived.
Instead you will be haunted by their words
that echo in the silence.
A job-stealing Alien. Not ever enough to be human,
forever silenced.
But I'm tired, tired of believing their lies,
feeding them to others
to disguise my despise.
We were made to be one nation under God.
Not one nation under a land.
Maybe I found that hard to understand.
I found the strength but not in the place I was looking for.
I felt like the odds were stacked against me
but love was on my side.
Our roots are what hold the tall tree.
Accepting who I am is what sets me free.

It is no longer winter, it is spring.
I accept my struggles are unique, but they are occurring.
So dear younger self,
You don't have to live in a self-perpetrated hell.
I spent so long trying to change you not realizing
I was the one that needed to change.
So take my hand and let me make this right.
Citizen or not, your future is bright.
Everyone wanted us to see we could not thrive.
So let's show them we could survive and strive.
I don't want to hide who I am!
¡No quiero esconder quien soy!
Learn to love myself and my struggles.
Aprender a amarme a mí misma y a mis luchas.
Es tiempo de cambiar, begin to live this life,
for I am blessed
And my heart will finally rest.

Janeth Melchor, Grade 11
Pacifica High School, Ventura County
Monique Cybulski, Classroom Teacher
Fernando Salinas, Poet Teacher

I Am an Only Child

I am an only child
I am as free as anyone can be
I feel like the main character in a great story
I feel like a cat, calm and feisty
I feel fine never having to share
Never having to fight
I am an only child
I feel peaceful, the house is always quiet
Just me playing the piano, singing
Throwing a ball against the wall
Watching my favorite shows
I am an only child
I feel like winter and summer combined
No break in seasons, no interruption
I feel like a cheetah running wild
No comparison, no competition

Ariana Rajvi Joshi, Grade 5
Mountain View Elementary, Santa Barbara County
Ciera Cote, Classroom Teacher
Cie Gumucio, Poet Teacher

A Moon Sleeping in the Sky Resting and Dreaming

My eyes are watery like a lake, whenever I cry.
My eyes are beautiful like a snake.
My hair is like the smooth fur of a tiger
with ruby gold and shininess.
My mouth is full when I talk like a bird chirping.
My thoughts are full of memories and love.
I become a moon resting up in the sky.
I dream of doing my future goals warming my world.
I wish I could one day reach a goal.
I miss the younger me laughing and jumping around.
Sometimes I feel like a moon sleeping in the sky resting
and dreaming while the sun goes up.

Jynelle Bungay, Grade 5
Longfellow Elementary, San Francisco County
Sheryl Carrillo, Classroom Teacher
Susan Terence, Poet Teacher

A Search for Belonging

I read the theme,
And the one word that stuck out to me
In big bold letters was

BELONGING

I wonder
Do I write what they want to hear–
All the lies that would make me out to be this perfect girl?
The one who fits in
and belongs
and looks like the picture-perfect magazine cover model?
Push down all my struggles, and
act like I am FINE

Stand tall,
and put on a smile
And when they ask me, "Are you okay?"
I nod my head and say 'm great!

No!

That is not who I am
or how I feel
I do not feel like I belong
The words begin to spit out,
like a nosebleed dripping down
Hands shaking,
tears flowing,
the truth comes out

I search for my roots, and
seek belonging
But this isn't my generation

I wish to not feel so alone
To find someone like me
Someone who listens to my type of music
Someone who watches UFC
And doesn't just know
The Notorious Conor McGregor
or Jon "Bones" Jones

I wonder maybe
if my interests weren't so different than others
It wouldn't be such a struggle to fit in
To belong

Why am I like this?

The whispers,
the laughs,
I know they are about me
I wish I lived in the 80s
The 80's seemed like a fantastic dream
Cell Phones weren't such a distraction
Friends communicated and
talked in person and not just on a screen
You rotated the dial of your phone
Clockwise, and worried about your parents
Listening to your conversations between your friends

You had a Walkman and listened to mixtapes
Mixtapes that had different themes
One for when you were sad
or when you had butterflies in your stomach
When love made you feel
like you were the main character in a movie

As I walk by myself,
just me and my thoughts alone
This question circles around my mind and linger,

like a buzzing bee near your ear all the time
Is it worth it to belong?
To the point you lose yourself
You look in the mirror and
you can no longer recognize who you are

Is it worth pretending to be someone who you are not?
Is it worth losing yourself in order to belong

Or

Is it better to be happy, to be at peace?
Take a deep breath, look at the beautiful sky
Even though you may not belong
You are happy
You are you
And that is unique

One day you'll find someone
Somebody who appreciates you
Who makes you feel as beautiful as a blue carnation
Someone who makes you laugh when you're crying
Someone who watches UFC, and
knows the happiness of the time
when Charles Oliveira got his belt
The pain of knowing Tony Ferguson is 0-7
The heartbreak you felt
when you saw Alexander Volkanovski
got knocked out by Illia Topuria
And they understand the reason why you always say, "Chama"

Somebody who makes you feel like you belong
Without having to change even one single thing about yourself
The puzzle piece that completes the picture

That's when you'll smile,
because you realize
You have finally found
A sense of belonging

Alysia Mikayla Clayton, Grade 11
Pacifica High School, Ventura County
Corrinne Abbott, Classroom Teacher
Fernando Salinas, Poet Teacher

A Normal Morning

An eye opens because of my mom.
Backpack loaded. Ready to go.
C was the answer. So that was why I got 99 marks.
Day almost done. Wait, I was so wrong. It has not been lunch.
Eating snack. Still thinking about home.
Finding my friends during recess.
Got my friends located.
Heading to them.
I said *sup*. They said *sup* too.
Just a normal recess.
Kate cheated on a test.
Lunch is finally here.
Munching on my nuggies.
No one dared to ask me to pet the cat on recess.
Oli stared at me all recess.
Phone got a text. It was my bestie.
Q was the hardest question but she got answers.
Ready for another test.
School is almost over.
iT has just ended.
bUs is here.
Vess texted me again.
What was the answer?
X and C were correct.
whY is Oli staring at me again?
Zzz, I slept on the bus.

Iris Conlan, Grade 2
Dow's Prairie Elementary, Humboldt County
Yasmin Reyes, Classroom Teacher
Dan Zev Levinson, Poet Teacher

Life Goes Up and Down

I am enchiladas that bring joy to big backs.
The best culture from Mexico,
My dad; nowhere to be found.
My mom; an independent woman.

I am Fideo soup that takes me back to my childhood;
The best birria tacos out there.
The sadness after elementary.

I am The Cardigans,
Alex G,
The best Mitski songs in the whole world.

I am the bouncing purple lowrider,
the smartest people, and friends that will be there,
but not for long.

I am my grandma's love for her grandchild,
Isn't it a nice view forever?
I am the trees that people chop down;
Life goes up and down like hills.

Katie Pichardo, Grade 7
San Fernando Middle School, Los Angeles County
David Malley, Classroom Teacher
Juan Cardenas, Poet Teacher

I Am a Girl

I am a girl in a small city
but I am a girl who feels like a
little marigold in a huge meadow.
I am a tiny silver star in
the big bright universe
but unlike the other stars
I am a star who cares for the Earth
a star who loves nature.
I am the gleam of angels' wings
but in heaven I am no different than any other
When I am on Earth
I am my own special human being
Just like everyone else.

Emma Scanlon, Grade 4
Lu Sutton Elementary, Marin County
Pamela Stuzman, Classroom Teacher
Michele Rivers, Poet Teacher

Solo Imagínalo

Si yo fuera una pequeña hoja bailando por el aire,
nunca me detendría y seguiría a mis amigos los pájaros.
Si yo fuera un pisa, un suelo de cemento,
simplemente descansando y siendo pisado por otros.
Si yo fuera un enorme gigante,
me comería las deliciosas nubes sabor chocolate.
Si yo fuera un árbol,
hablaría con los animales ye los animaría.
Si yo fuera un poderoso oso,
no le tendría miedo a nada y me andaría paseando por ahí.
No lo sobre pienses, solo imagina.

Just Imagine It

If I were a tiny leaf dancing through the air,
I would never stop and I would follow my friends, the birds.
If I were a floor I would be a cement floor,
simply resting and being stepped on by others.
If I were an enormous giant,
I would eat the delicious chocolate flavored clouds.
If I were a tree I would speak with the animals,
and I would encourage them.
If I were a powerful bear,
I would not be afraid of anything and I would go walking about.
Don't overthink it. Just imagine.

Iyari Bañuelos, Grade 6
Translated by Jaqueline Lopez
Roseland Elementary, Sonoma County
Madeline Salonga, Classroom Teacher
Lisa Shulman, Poet Teacher

I Write Beautiful

I write like a cat purring away, today-now or never.
I write like a peacock,
no time to delay-spread out my feathers,
impress-rest.
I write like a diamond, pretty, gleam-I need to be seen.
I write like a phoenix, golden, fly, rebirth and die, again I try.
I write like an otter, small, mighty, kind, rewind.
I write like a weeping willow, only I don't cry,
nor try to be a liar, thief,
no one can catch me.
I write like the ground that keeps you standing,
and you land, landing.
I write like the Earth's heart, beautifully smart.
I write like a butterfly, fly, not on butter, my life I don't mutter.
I write the words inside my head,
poems, stories, songs, green lawns?
I write what no one can understand,
except me, my writing is not
messy, it's what I see, think of it, it's all me.
I write like it's alive, coming toward me,
bringing me into its shade,
glory, I see its story.
I write like the feeling it brings, joy,
and many other things, coming and
going, feeling alive, mine.
I write beautifully, don't you agree?

Tirza Kinports, Grade 4
Hope Elementary, Santa Barbara County
Isao Sugano, Classroom Teacher
Cie Gumucio, Poet Teacher

Complex Circle

I used to be a dense book
Stuck high up on the shelf
Closed, Unknowing, and Full
But now I am the burst of air
That turns pages
Coasting any open story
I used to be a mirror
Laid down on the ground
Until a step too heavy
I cracked
Now I am a newborn
Starting over again
I was a circle for a brain
Now my skeleton is a spiral

Rewster Blackburn, Grade 11
Community Pacific Charter, Mendocino County
Whitney Badget, Classroom Teacher
Blake More, Poet Teacher

My Heart Loves and Hates

My heart loves my sister
my heart hates when she screams

My heart loves the Earth
my heart hates when people hurt it

My heart loves people
my heart hates mean people

My heart loves every skin color
my heart hates racism

My heart loves dreams
my heart hates nightmares

My heart loves kindness
my heart hates meanness

My heart loves air
my heart hates pollution

I love my heart

Riley Hornsby, 5th Grade
Cutten Elementary, Humboldt County
Mindi Bon, Classroom Teacher
Dan Zev Levinson, Poet Teacher

Star Child

Raised by wolves,
I always felt
too small for my body.
Praised
as the star child,
my teeth
always tasted of iron.
But these ears of mine
feel too small,
and these guts of mine,
unholy.
So when the hunters
find me in the snow,
they'll cut me open for warmth.
And they'll be
shocked to find
the rabbit
that lives beneath
the skin of the star child.

Samantha Lazaro, Grade 11
Willits High School, Mendocino County
Katrina Hall, Classroom Teacher
J.W. Churchill, Poet Teacher

A Life

I am a mournful survivor
But I wish I weren't
They left me alive
But I wish I weren't
My mother, life blotted out by Japanese invaders
Right before my disbelieving eyes
My beautiful Toisan, burning, deserted

Tell me a story
To convince me that life is worth living
A golden mountain, halfway across the world
I am the will to survive, iron determination
Runs strong in my veins
I ride the ship to freedom, to new life
to hope
That I can be whole again

I am the deceived
Lured and captured
With the promise of freedom
So tangible on my tongue
Tantalizing, yet so far away
Angel Island, a treacherous contradicting label
For the demons who oversee the
candle in my heart slowly giving out

I've felt worse
Finally liberated from the suffocating air of the prison
A new land,
strangers who don't know the comforting dialect of my home

I am the welder in the shipyard
of the dazzling San Francisco Bay
Metal and sound all around
Lonely, but it is more than nothing

I can Hope again
Happiness has taken pity on me
The love of my life, here with me at last
I am the small laundromat on the corner of
Flowery Detergent and background humming
We toil, never-ending, mounds of laundry

Kira Feng, Grade 9
Lowell High School, San Francisco County
Mitchell Feingold, Classroom Teacher
Susan Terence, Poet Teacher

Cover

I am a book on the shelves of the Ortega Library
surrounded by many others
not standing out

I sit there quietly, waiting to be picked
Waiting for my smooth surfaced, waxy cover to be noticed
People walk by and stare as I sit here

I'm colorful, am I not?
And interesting, may I add
So why won't I be chosen?

I have all sorts of colors you see!
Shades blending into each other
Why am I still sitting here?

Just take a look inside!
I'm interesting I promise!
My story tells so!
You can't tell from the cover alone-

"You can't tell from the cover alone."

I see,
I'm more than just
my cover.

I want to be picked for my story,
For what I really am
For who I really am

The cover is all for show,
It's not the real me
So why must I be judged for it so?

Ash Goldenberg, Grade 9
Lowell High School, San Francisco County
Christian Villanueva, Classroom Teacher
Susan Terence, Poet Teacher

Baseball

When I wear the baseball cleats of confidence I can run
As fast as a cheetah.
When I wear the batting gloves of power I can hit
2 homeruns.
When I wear the black, Nike glove I can get 13 strikeouts.
I win the game with a walk-off grand slam.

Patrick Robinson, Grade 4
Alexander Valley Elementary, Sonoma County
Nadia Podesto, Classroom Teacher
Maureen Hurley, Poet Teacher

Let Time Pass

I used to be easy and simple to solve
But now I'm complex and question what I am

I used to be excited to grow up and become an adult
But now I hope to once again become a kid

I used to think that fame was the main goal
But now I only crave peace

I used to ignore my surroundings
But now wherever I go I look at every detail around me.

I used to hate the chilly nights and would rather sleep
But now when I get the chance
I gaze upon the infinite stars upon me

I used to hate listening to music
because I thought it was too girly
But now I can't stop listening to addictive beats.

I used to hate the Mexican beans my parents made for dinner
But now I happily eat every last bite

I used to question my future and how it will go
But now I just let time pass and wait for the time to come

I used to despise change and thought it wasn't important
But now I realize that change is good and necessary for growth.

Christopher Cadena, Grade 8
Manchester School, Mendocino County
Avis Anderson, Classroom Teacher
Blake More, Poet Teacher

Special Glasses

(a mash-up poem)

Last night
the rain
spoke to me
fast, furious
equal to different things I'm in luck because
I have special glasses
partial for good or bad things
Solar Eclipse
I am a joyful person
I am a football person
I am a boy
I'm the sun bright and shining person
I'm a chill
I'm a kind person and friend
I'm love but for my mom
I have a big personality
I have loving parents
My favorite thing
is playing sports
in the California sunshine
My favorite things
are playing basketball and football
Playing
with friends
Prodigy
I am a seal
I am a brown seal

I sleep underwater
I eat krill I'm Michael Jordan I'm a
professional basketball
player for the Bulls

Gavin Dixon, Grade 3
Chenoweth Elementary, Merced County
Meuy Saeteurn, Classroom Teacher
Dawn Trook, Poet Teacher

First Time Reader

She stages.
Metal doors sing a cacophony of screeches as they open,
Chubby feet already toddling forward
Kissing the ash carpet of Floor Five.
The mother falls behind,
Novels from a trip to the stacks towering, sweating sentences.
(It is too late.)
Stubby fingers stun the length of an eggshell wall
with grease and grime,
Pillowy mire caked under ragged nails.
And it's there, in the distance:
A minute, scarlet box mounted neatly
at the very end of the hallway,
A shiny silver lock the cherry on top.
As the tot teeters forward in pursuit of the crimson enigma,
Realization dawns: there are letters on the box,
and they have meaning.
Always a rule-follower, she obeys the words.
Three firemen and fifty-two disgruntled evacuations later,
She learns the significance of "Pull Here."

Naomi Ko, Grade 12
St. Ignatius College Preparatory, San Francisco County
Jacqueline Boland, Classroom Teacher
Maxine Flasher-Düzgüneş, Poet Teacher

Olive Tree

Blinding and beautiful sun that dwindled in an orange sky
Passing an ancient olive tree, its fickle bark twisted and torn,
oozing centuries of history
Blade-like leaves shimmer in Sol's afternoon splendor
as they cut through the dusty zephyr
Green ovoid fruit anointed with kingly oil
plucked unceremoniously and brought to my lips
Overwhelming bitterness
Gravel shifting and fitting together under my feet
destroying any semblance of its personal
space
I ascend a dirt trail, earth swirling,
stepping over the fragments of my people
Dull rocks tell a tale as old as time
Ancient shards of pottery that cut my inner being
Terracotta puzzle
The land of my people, where archaic memories choose to dwell
Centuries of nomadic wandering, enslavement, banishment, exile
A people steeped with ancient scrolls and songs
The hope to return, a desire to persist, the need for peace
Dove clutching an olive branch – a symbol of our timeless quest
Branches break, roots hold fast, a testament to our steadfast past
Birds chirping, bullets whistling,
deafening thunder, explosive lightning
Shrapnel rain
Olive skinned grandmother scavenges and picks at the bone
I scavenged old bones — the pieces of a long-forgotten era
When prophets roamed
My roots, my people
An olive tree with a thick bark, deep roots, and bitter fruits
Memories of the past and the present converge
I walk over the fragments of a lost soul's life

Smashed pottery, smashed home
I try and escape the realities of an ongoing era
We didn't belong before, and we don't belong now
What will be left to scavenge of my people?
Ancient temples and pottery
Smashed homes and picture frames
The price to pay for my selfish wanting;
Selfish desire to dream of belonging
Cost an arm and a leg
For some people.

Jack Byrett, Grade 11
Adolfo Camarillo High School, Ventura County
Heidi Resnik, Classroom Teacher
Fernando Salinas, Poet Teacher

The Artist

(a mash-up poem)

I am a sky showing the Earth my true beauty.
I jump in the puddles that the rain has gifted us.
I am purple being super duper fearless.
Red is for love.
California is where people walk their dogs.
Some eclipses are about the moon and others are about
the sun, all eclipses are unseeable.
I am an American Artist that's known for my art.

Sofia Rojas, Grade 3
Chenoweth Elementary, Merced County
Amy Brown, Classroom Teacher
Dawn Trook, Poet Teacher

Wheel Of Justice

My heart wants to go to space.
If I do, it will float away.
My heart is good at jumping around
In my body. My heart is a wheel of
Justice making sure nothing goes wrong.
My heart is as black as can be. My
heart is as crazy as an eagle when I see my
Grandma.

Giancarlo Jimenez, Grade 4
Alexander Valley Elementary, Sonoma County
Nadia Podesto, Classroom Teacher
Maureen Hurley, Poet Teacher

In My Little World

I enjoy ballet dancing
mainly in summer
and warm peaceful days
I love it because of the cool breeze
when I turn or the swift feeling
when I glide across the floor
in the afternoon in Middletown
is where I stay
I love dancing and hearing the sounds
of pointe shoes tapping on the floor
or the calm and restful music
until the clock strikes four
I'm in my little world
not worrying about anything
anymore

Lucia Ferguson, Grade 5
Cobb Elementary, Lake County
Natasha McKenney, Classroom Teacher
Michele Krueger, Poet Teacher

People of the Rainbow

Blue, Green, Pink, Yellow, Brown
Splattered on my face
People look at me
I know they wonder about my race
Purple, Orange, Black, Red, White
Splattered on my face
More people look at me
Now it's a race
A race to guess what my race is
I can't breathe
Hands covering my face
I need space
But I am being chased
I have eyes, hair, hands, feelings
Everything other people have
But when they look at me
They are still fazed
What is so wrong about my race?

Jasmine Guerrero Sevilla, Grade 12
Santa Ynez Valley Union High School, Santa Barbara County
Melanie Dickey, Classroom Teacher
Cie Gumucio and Michelle Pitttenger, Poet Teachers

Who I Am

Sometimes, I am a sword,
made of sunlight,
with a shining golden light,
that penetrates all difficulties.

Sometimes, I am a shield,
condensed by moonlight,
shining with a hint of brilliant silver light,
to resist all suffering.

Sometimes, I am a gust of cold wind,
that brings the biting ice,
passing through certain places,
but doesn't stop.

Sometimes, I am a rotten bird,
with a heart with a hint of warmth,
wandering beside the Oriental Pearl Tower,
lost in a forest made of steel,
that is shining with a strange light.

Most of the time, I am just a lake,
not pleased, not to have compassion,
like a mirror that reflects everything around me.
And use my emerald green lake water,
mercilessly devouring everyone,
that wants to seek inside the bitingly cold lake.

Frank Li, Grade 9
Lowell High School, San Francisco County
Mitch Feingold, Classroom Teacher
Susan Terence, Poet Teacher

Inner Worlds,
Questions and
Imaginations

Paper

I am paper scribbled, thin, ripped a little, and doodled
I have cats, dogs, and superheroes on me
I am sometimes junk, but sometimes important
On the inside, I am a hawk which soars high
Searching for prey up high where I have never been
Up in the mountains with cool air, the clouds
And never seen things
I am a hawk on the inside
I wish to fly with others up high where snow lies far away
I feel lost and lonely as junk,
But I have a twinge of greatness when I am important
I am usually white but sometimes,
Colored on
I know all secret notes and what is written on them
But my dream is to become a hawk,
Happy and high

Mihika Wagner, Grade 4/5 (combo)
Mountain View Elementary, Santa Barbara County
Ciera Cote, Classroom Teacher
Cie Gumucio, Poet Teacher

My Heart's Desire

My heart has a desire, a desire to write.
My heart has a bucket list as long as the park.
My heart has a desire to have great friends
and to be with you for everything.
My heart has a desire to be smart
and help me through hard times.
My heart has a desire to save people.
My heart needs freedom
and thinking room to be smart.
My heart has a desire to finish its bucket list.
If my heart played a sport it would play hockey
and it would be a goalie.
It could save peoples opportunities
because my heart has a desire to save the world.

Ella Rotlisberger, Grade 4
Alexander Valley Elementary, Sonoma County
Nadia Podesto, Classroom Teacher
Maureen Hurley, Poet Teacher

Buzzing Brass

Anxiety is BUZZing in my head
like an orange bass playing fast
as I step on stage.
What will he say? What will she say?
Will they laugh?
Will the rushing river of thoughts
come out with all my pride?
(The weather that day was on and off
just like anxiety.)
I'm an anxious ticking time bomb.
Am I spreading this?
"Ew, she's contagious!"
When is this due? I- I-
bet anxiety knows.
Can I go back home to warm cookies?
No No No No.
Anxiety, Anxiety, you're too deep.
No going back when you hear
bells ringing.
It is so hard to find the...well,
whatever. Never mind.

Olympia Arrow Justice Reeder, Grade 4
Park Elementary, Marin County
Leslie Bernstein, Classroom Teacher
Claire Blotter, Poet Teacher

Doors

When you open my muddy grass door you'll see an extraordinary water slide made of an old baseball bat and a mitt as a canoe. You will play bowling with my rusty helmet and knock over caged fences. If you finish everything you will see a sliding glass player open up into my next imagination, the world of Legos. Brick stairs leading up to a molten lava volcano where useless bricks can be melted and turned into some other kids' wild creation. However, if someone like you jumps into the monstrosity you will be transported to the world of vanilla. The silk-like ground is made up of a cream-colored icing and ice cream sandwiches. The sea is the flavor itself and the boats are made of cake with the smallest bit of chocolate. You can sail to your final destination, the world of memories. You can see yourself and all the good things you've done and what you can improve on. Your sister falling over and you helping her up, the way you cared for your dog that passed away all those years ago. At the end of the hallway you see yourself and how you've improved over your lifetime.

Baron Smith, Grade 5
Mountain View Elementary, Santa Barbara County
Nate Latta, Classroom Teacher
Cie Gumucio, Poet Teacher

Facing

I suppose every face tells a story
That dent in my mother's might be where I bit her,
Feverish, young; I don't remember doing it, just regretting it.
Or suspiciously similar to the place I just picked off
In some hotel room, at one, too tired to resist.

I guess they are about as forgiving as life is with mistakes.
That acne might blow over, even though I didn't wash yesterday
Anything I do might not matter, anyway:
Faces and people die together.
But somehow, for this moment,
how it feels and looks matters practically.

Also, there's race, of course
Isn't it a funny word, like we are running down a track, sweating
And somehow the color of what's sweating
Matters to how hugs are doled out at the end of the mile
Or doesn't, because you can't see it; you've money for facials

So, there's money, whether you can,
Or are interested in showing you can,
Spend thirty minutes a night rubbing creams,
But never be able to change the fundamental shape;
The kind smile you haven't got, so it doesn't matter anyway.

Yes, that smile's the real story, or
Whether you're weathered from the outdoors
Or dedicate so much to One Love you don't shower
But still pinch the cheeks and show the oil run out
Just to demonstrate you once might've cared,
and know something of life.

Frej Barty, Grade 11
Mendocino High School, Mendocino County
Sam Stump, Classroom Teacher
Blake More, Poet Teacher

It's Raining Tacos!

Taco! Monday! Taco! Tuesday! Taco! Wednesday!
Taco! Thursday! Taco! Friday! Taco! Saturday!
Taco! Sunday! Wrapped inside a piping hot tortilla!
Tacos! Ooozing with flavorful meat and salsa!
Tacos! Friends with jalapenos! Tacos!
Look like semi-circles! Tacos!
A mega lunch of tantalizing flavor! Tacos!
Crunch! Crunch! Spicy fire! Tacos!
Game day food suggestion! Tacos!
It's raining tacos! Tsunami of spice! Tacos!
What's the best food?! Tacos!
Tacos! Tacos!

Asher Kim, Grade 4
Edna McGuire Elementary, Marin County
Aimee Levin, Classroom Teacher
Claire Blotter, Poet Teacher

Dystopia(n)

As I lay to put myself to sleep,
my body is restless and my mind,
ill at ease.
For I find myself
trembling, aching, sweating beads.
I crave the light.

And not the deranged luminescence
that runs rampant through the town.
Aggressively putting down
all else that attempts to
shed the city of its nighttime cloak.
The light above which fades out and drowns,
suffering because of it.

Nor that light which is swallowed.
Vital for life,
though I refuse to swallow that pill.
I can survive without it.

But rather,
the light of my screen.
Dopamine and pings.
I can stop whenever I want.
This radiant glow
illuminates my fears,
keeping my dreams in the shadows.

Enlightenment to what end?
Schooling to be counteracted by Zombieland.
A ravenous pit of terror and terrifying light.

A moth,
I come to life in the night.
Attention seized
by the dark side of light.
A pocket-sized,

apocalypse-
inducing blaze,
hidden behind
the veil of cracked glass
and a phone case.

Kieran Lundy, Grade 8
Hughes Middle School, Los Angeles County
Nancy Woo, Poet Teacher

Life

How come so many people talk about the colors in the skies
and no one ever writes about the teardrops in their eyes
I've never written about the effects it has on my mind
Has anybody ever looked at you with eyes of stone?
I've thought about how different life would be
but I'm afraid that the wrong move will separate us
Sometimes the idea of darkness is still there
other times I'm inspired by the people around me
Why is it no one dreams of what the world could be?
Have you heard about life without lies?
Maybe if you changed the way you acted things would be different
Does anyone know what they do affects the people around them?
No one ever told me what happened, but I still know
Maybe you can help me solve all these riddles laid out by adults
who are too scared of the truth
Tell me how this works in your mind?
Does it impact the way you see me
or the way you see everyone else?

Seraphine Ries, Grade 7
Mendocino K-8 School, Mendocino County
Aimee Frederick, Classroom Teacher
Blake More, Poet Teacher

The Colors of Happiness

My soul wants the color of happiness,
love and joy filling me up.
My soul is not afraid of darkness
My soul is strong, it dreams
of no more sadness left in the world.
My soul wishes to help
to save all those in need.
My soul wants to feed the poor.
My soul wants to travel to the island of joy.

Valentina Saini, Grade 4
Alexander Valley Elementary, Sonoma County
Nadia Podesto, Classroom Teacher
Maureen Hurley, Poet Teacher

Somewhere

My feeling is a tie-dye alien with a sassy attitude
and no friends with antennas on its head and feet
and arms, the shape of antennas.

My feeling is the shape of a kidney bean covering
the white page alone like a statue in pale light.

My feeling moves like a soft stone
always changing its mind and just moving
in the wind but then stopping as soon as
it changes its mind once more.

My feeling pictures a mean girl making fun of it
by saying what my feeling says in a mean way.

My feeling sees a pretty field with one flower there,
the grass around her seems like it is saying,
ha ha in the wind.

Ellison McLean, Grade 3
Loma Verde Elementary, Marin County
Brenda Pfeifer, Classroom Teacher
Claire Blotter, Poet Teacher

A Planet of Platitudes

What's a person to do
amidst so many platitudes?
How can we know what's real?
What's so?

I ask sincerely:
Where, on Earth,
did authenticity go?

Is it floating somewhere
in the sea?
Caught in a fishing net
of ambiguity?
Or perhaps lost
across vast canyons
of polarity?

Wherever it is,
I admit,
the uncertainty
sometimes gets to me.
And I confess,
leaves me speechless.

What if,
instead,
we return
to speaking
in the language of moments,
in the tongue of laughter,
in the dialectic of tears?

Our words
would be worlds

---

would be inseparable
from action.
They would take effort
and their purpose would be full.

I say
let's leave
this planet of platitudes.
Move to a universe
where our verses are verbs
And our adjectives are allegories.

No matter how our voices might
roll on the r,
cut the q,
or twist the w,
we all understand
the urge
to live in the moment
and just be
and be carefree.

But, you see,
especially
given all the challenges
of the day,
It's not enough for our actions
to be conscious,
deliberate,
and
brave.

Even though the saying goes:
"Actions speak louder than words,"
words, too, have sway.
They act upon us,
and within us.

They begin in the body.
They shape our brains,
and stretch our lips.

I'm not speaking about body language.
Or even language of the body.

What I'm saying is this:
Through language,
we can embody
the change we want to make.
But we must speak from the heart
and do our part
to choose our words
mindfully.

However much we may wish to speak
and do as we please,
you and me,
can we finally agree,
that what we do
affects others too?

This knowledge doesn't have to be
a burden we all carry.
We don't have to live weary.

Let's recognize each chuckle
as a syllable,
each guffaw
a rhyme,
let every love
be a story,
and platitudes
a crime.

After all,
what does the modern ear hear
in the sonnets of Shakespeare?
For today's writers and lovers,
is love still as deep as the sea?
Is their bounty as boundless?
If not, can it be?

If so, I believe
we must pay more attention
to words,
not only what we do to them,
but what they do to us -
physically.

And let's not forget about silence.
For the absence of sound
shapes us too.
Silence creates space
inside us,
where we can hear
what's actually being said.

So, let's act more honorably
and choose our words
more carefully.
In a time
when what matters
often remains unseen,
let's take time
to say what we mean.

Let's speak out.
Create an honest symposium
of sound
as we gather round.
Let's listen closely,

ears pressed to the ground,
to the floor.
Let's open the doors
of our minds
and make our world more
like we imagine it can be.

Our future
lies in our language,
lives in our bodies
and lingers in our souls.

If we embrace
the undeniable corporality
of our words
and our world,
we can
change our mentality.

Truth is,
it's possible
we need poetry
just as much
as practicality.

Ruby Kosek, Grade 11
Tamalpais High School, Marin County
Michael Levinson, Classroom Teacher
Maxine Flasher-Düzgüneş, Poet Teacher

Salt Cricket

Flicker and twitch,
appendages of bygone flight.
They draped your body,
in a stretch of lustrous silk.
Around you:
Mournful incarnate.

I promised not to cry,
salt cricket.
"Leave your sorrows here with me."
You crystalized my tears,
and hid them under rigid flesh.

As I grew, I folded yours into mine.
Rubbed my guileless palms together.
Eroded you: bitter mineral,
to saline integument.

Rougher hands,
cast in a thick shell of brine.
No longer grasp at the fleeting grail.

When are you coming home?
Salt cricket,
I'm waiting on porch steps.
Though it was me, in my haste,
Who maimed your cherished wings.

Reaching for the mountain's skyline,
my brackish tears drip,
like candle wax,
upon my salt-born sepulcher.

Cade Palmer, Grade 12
Marin School of the Arts, Marin County
Rebecca Pollack, Classroom Teacher,
Maxine Flasher-Düzgüneş, Poet Teacher

How Do I Believe?

How do I believe when my
world is a mirage?
How do I believe when
the things I care for
die?
Even though everything has
a life cycle, I just can't seem
to accept that they're all
gone.
When I die, I am not sure
what to expect.
All I know is that
everyone I care for
will be with me.

I suppose I should be
mad at Death for taking
everyone. But they will
be proud of me if I continue
on, all of their spirits lift
me onto their shoulders,
waiting for me to fulfill
my destiny.

Annabelle Littlefield, Grade 5
Freshwater Elementary, Humboldt County
Dara Soto, Classroom Teacher
Dan Zev Levinson, Poet Teacher

Death

Death is silent like you
sleeping in the night
Death is black like darkness
Death is peaceful like the moon
Death is scary
Death is not the end
but a new beginning
Death is silent like blood
Death is pure darkness
Death is a shadow seeking revenge
Death leads to silence and horror
Death is scary, that's okay
Your soul will fly
and live like no other
You will be Death
I will be Death
I will live in your heart
You will live in mine

Bowie Perego-Saldana, Grade 3
Montecito Union Elementary, Santa Barbara County
Jacki Hammer, Classroom Teacher
Kimbrough Ernest, Poet Teacher

Space in My Heart

The lost piece of the puzzle
is what my heart aches for,
it aches to be whole. My heart
feels full of misinformation as fake
creativity fills the empty hole,
the emotions that hear my tears.

My heart is the vast forest
full of tourists bashing through all
the constructive creativity that should
fill the inattentive space . . .

My heart feels unwhole.

Gage Mitchell, Grade 6
Skyfish School, Humboldt County
Lucia Setyowati & Teal Cyrek, Classroom Teachers
Dan Zev Levinson, Poet Teacher

Forgiveness is Freedom

Forgiveness is unchaining my soul, unburdening me.
Forgiveness is love, no longer fighting against anger
Ending the argument.
Forgiveness is handing someone the key to my heart.
Anger comes from a lack of forgiveness.
It is a fake smile.
A whispered word.
A stab in the back, reaching through to the heart
Anger can be exchanged in wordless eye contact
or in glares of rage.
Forgiveness is like the sun rising
Leaving behind the dark night of anger
Letting all the frustrations seep away into brilliant bright light.
Forgiveness is letting go
Admitting mistakes were made.
Leaving myself open like a diary.
Forgiveness is like weeding,
letting light through to the flowers and watching them grow.
Forgiveness is freedom.

Hazel Maxwell, Grade 6
Mill Valley Middle School, Marin County
Bethany Bloomston, Classroom Teacher
Michele Rivers, Poet Teacher

The Inside Place

The heart inside is a
huge place.
The trees
surround my lake
of life.
The foxes and
unicorns and
dragons
protect my lake of life.
The
lake of life
sparkles with memories.
When I sleep,
I dip my body in
and let the memories
and dreams
coat me, like a
skin of flower petals.
My heart is where I go
when life doesn't make sense,
to live the chill life,
to make up for everything
wrong in the world.
My lake of life in my heart in my head in my happiness.

Lily Gardner, Grade 5
Arcata Elementary, Humboldt County
Nicole Reis, Classroom Teacher
Dan Zev Levinson, Poet Teacher

The Void

Beyond the world, there is a void.
A void of mist, and death.
An ocean of fire and ice,
cold, and nothingness.
But in the fog you see a cherry tree
With pink flowers, on an island.
As you began to feel hopeful, the mist clears
revealing a world beyond this world.
Your doubt has clouded your vision,
obscuring the rest of the universe.
But now you see clearly,
And you are free.

Isabel Sutro, Grade 4
Alexander Valley Elementary, Sonoma County
Nadia Podesto, Classroom Teacher
Maureen Hurley, Poet Teacher

The Fire Deep Inside

Love is the fire deep inside of you
Waiting to come out of the shadows
Until dives back down like a dolphin
And coming back up from the watery depths.

Isaiah St. Clair, Grade 4
Alexander Valley Elementary, Sonoma County
Nadia Podesto, Classroom Teacher
Maureen Hurley, Poet Teacher

Flying Heart

My heart is longing for flight.
I just want to be like a kite.
I want to be on that runway.
I want to start my heart.
I'm longing for the freeing feeling.
Over the highest buildings.
My heart wants to press through the clouds.
I'm flying into the sun.

Parker O'Hara, Grade 5
Morris Elementary, Humboldt County
Kendra Inzer, Classroom Teacher
Dan Zev Levinson, Poet Teacher

Atychiphobia

How come so few people talk about
the fear that comes with failure
and no one ever writes about
the overhead looming guilt of it all
I've never written about
the feeling of needing to be perfect
has anyone ever
truly won or been the best at everything
I've thought about
how to win it all
but I'm afraid
to lose and see how far I fall
Sometimes, the idea
of people not having faith in me
makes my bones break
Other times I'm inspired
to prove them wrong
and show the steps I take
Why is it no one dreams
of just being mediocre
Have you heard of
being a perfectionist
maybe if you
were humbled by losing
you wouldn't be so scared
Does anyone know
the real point of victory
No one ever told me
so now I shake when I'm not winning
Maybe you can help me
by showing me the truth
tell me

Will you pity me when I lose
Does it
make you unsure
of what to do?

Melea Garner, Grade 7
Mendocino K-8 School, Mendocino County
Aimee Frederick, Classroom Teacher
Blake More, Poet Teacher

A Song Written by God

5,6,7,8
First position,
plié
Second position,
plié
Fourth & Fifth,
plié then relevé
ballet slippers sweep the floor
heels turned out
en pointe
shoulders down,
elbows, chin, and chest lifted

our moves follow the tempo
a soft tune plays
I chasse,
step,
step,

then grand jeté onto the shore
where the gentle cymbals of the waves
meet with the golden grains
the ocean breeze dancing through
the midnight strands of my hair

each wave and curl flowing from my roots
like the grooves on a vinyl
playing the song of my heartstrings
plucking each note
with the heart beating
of the needle of my sewing machine
stitching florals and gingham and waffle-knits with bows

---

as the ones on my soft-leather flats
to spin and pirouette
like the handle of a music box
inside holds a porcelain ballerina
forever elegant through music
elegance in my prayers
careful with each word
for kind words are like honey-
sweet to the soul and healthy for the body

and there stands my God by my side
the way and the truth and the life
for He is a beacon of light
as I dance through
the merry-go-round of life

the Producer of my song
He hand-picked each instrument
and played a melody

each quarter note and crescendo
each measure and rest
its volume more piano than forte
a harmony of brass, percussion, & winds
composed by God
Fearfully and Wonderfully made
a song titled Angelica

Angelica Magnaye, Grade 9
Del Sol High School, Ventura County
Eric Ehlers & Mona Piñon, Classroom Teachers
Fernando Salinas, Poet Teacher

Anger is Like a Book

Anger is like a book,
don't judge yourself from the outside,
but from inside.
Life is like a movie, it ends.
But there is always another one waiting for you.
Life is like a forest, so big,
like the challenges you can face.
Life is like a mirror, you see yourself
in it and judge yourself. Don't.
Life is like a city. So many friends
and you don't know which to keep.
Life is like the fire gone mad like the mind,
but don't trust it.
Life is like the sunrise,
every day, a new start.

Avery Monson, Grade 4
Alexander Valley Elementary, Sonoma County
Nadia Podesto, Classroom Teacher
Maureen Hurley, Poet Teacher

Pendant of Tears

In the abyss of uncertainty, I confront reality,
Your gaze holds tears on my chilled cheek,
A picture on the fridge, a memory untold,
Of a love whose name I've yet to behold.

I bear this pendant, tears woven in cloth,
A stain, a mark of a secret oath,
No ritual can restore what once was,
A love now faded, a painful loss.

Those sapphire eyes haunt like a bird in flight,
As you depart, promising to come back, but never in sight,
Your hands reach out, filled with sorrow,
But I can't reciprocate, our bond now hollow.

Lost in a haze of blue, I drift,
Facing oblivion, where home is stripped,
I wear this pendant, a mirror to my pain,
Cursed by a spell, my dreams in vain.

Lights shine bright, yet darkness reigns within,
My cries echo, my heart pleading to break free from this sin,
Each tear, a reminder of love gone sour,
As I yearn for the touch of a father's power.

Ice-cold tears, needles on my skin,
In the bathroom mirror, fog thickens within,
Moonlight pierces, revealing a soul's plight,
A spirit lost, unable to find its light.

Wearing this pendant of tears around my neck,
such a burden to bear,
Stained like the windows of a pious cathedral lair,
My heart aches for a father's embrace,
But all that remains, is an empty space.

In the sanatoriums embrace, I lay,
Preferable to the chains of familial dismay,
Watching you leave, onto familiar floors,
I wear this pendant of tears nevermore.

Giselle Carter, Grade 10
Adolfo Camarillo High School, Ventura County
Daryl Myers, Classroom Teacher
Fernando Salinas, Poet Teacher

Poet Teacher Poems

Poetry Afternoon at the Asylum House

In this underground shelter where questions—
regarding reasons for departure,
details of journeys— are avoided,
we start with the innocuous,
the acrostic of names.

There is nine-year-old Tatiana,
T for *Tengo miedo de perder mi familia,*
I am afraid of losing my family.
Teenage Lucero
whose name means light,
an evening star blazing the way,
begins with E for *Estoy triste,*
I'm sad;
O for *Otra vez empezando de nuevo,*
Once again, starting all over.

After the acrostic,
there are free verse laments
for pets left behind,
a *tía* lost to the bite of a scorpion;
and a poem about a peach,
which is really about the giver of the peach
who picked it as a gift for his girlfriend,
the poet's mother,
although the gangs got to him first
matandolo con gasolina,
setting him aflame with gasoline.

These kids are the lucky ones
who crossed the border
during a space of grace
in-between separated families

---

and turned-back asylees,
their claims deemed deserving.

They arrive at the asylum house
in armored ICE vans, their parents
bejeweled in ankle bracelet monitors.
In the dormitory, they wait
days or weeks
for their names to appear
on a list beside a new city, unpronounceable,
an agency unknown
that's agreed to resettle them.

On the lobby television,
the day's news trickles in,
the familiar horrors there—
a kidnapping in Mexico,
an activist assassination in Honduras.
And the unimagined ones here—
a factory raid in Mississippi,
children coming home from school
to empty houses;
another death in detention.

For our group emotion poem,
Brayan, age 10, proposes happiness.
Felicidad es mi familia,
he offers. *Es fútbol,* adds another.
And then-- *es helado*, ice cream,
es salir a jugar, to go out to play.
Felicidad, Brayan concludes for us,
es para todos, is for everyone.

On a crinkled piece of binder paper,
I weave together their words,
as if, by doing so,
I might cast some spell

to blast off their parents' monitors,
break down the walls from this subterranean shelter.
As if with our poems we might
rewrite this off-kilter world, tilt
and right it toward the light.

Lea Aschkenas
Poet Teacher, Marin County

Once the Red Carpet

I was once
I was her
I was hope
I was

I walked and wore
and looked a part
I hoped a walk
I'd walk the red carpet

I was once
I was her
I was hope
And I walked

And those paths
took me places
I can show you tracks and traces
Loops and lights
Beds and creeksides

And the light
The loops and light

I was once
I was her
I was hope
I am

And I walked
and found places
In many faces
And found fame
In blue blue light

Hopes they changed
to chance

I was once
I was her
I was hope
I am

I walk the land
No painted backdrops
My dreams they fall
as almond blossoms
my carpet

my fortune's rainwater
feeding creeks

I am once
I am her
I am hope
I am

Dawn Trook
Poet Teacher, Merced County

Poem Inspired by DCastro's Painting *The Sunset*

Three generations of African women
clap to the sunset, sing soprano
to the elephant in the golden sky
whose huge (varying shades of blue) tusk
encircles a loft of lavender, plum
and violet stars assembled
above, below, and beyond
our perspective.

Open-armed, kelly green, organ pipe cacti
accompany the clapping women,
an exquisite ensemble, with voices as textured
and vibrant as the complementary-colored
red and green, yellow and purple coverings
the Walamo women wear.

DCastro's *The Sunset* - a juxtaposition
of the visible and invisible;
desert cacti, serenading bush women,
villager ancestors, spirited elders, youth,
and the not-yet-born

who all sing in harmony
about an imagined world
resplendent with fertility and future
where harmony and love reside
where harmony and love reign.

Johnnierenee Nelson
Poet Teacher, San Diego County

Would You Call It Bravery?

Would you call it bravery to walk in
Sonoran Desert heat from June
through July and every month
thereafter even through lightning
storms and resulting monsoon floods
streets becoming once in a lifetime oceans

She wheeled the rusting shopping
cart from whatever store
she'd walked to—
despite my protests—
"Mom, you can't
take the shopping
cart home with you"

So I joined her, slinging
heavy cloth bags
of groceries over my arms
sweat rolling down
my forehead
burning my eyes

"See, would've been
easier with the shopping cart"
as asphalt burned through
soles of our tennis shoes

Bravery to live poor
not bemoan it
but to
adjust to day-old
week wizened
groceries

cutting flowering mold
off bread
using bath water
to wash floors
wash clothes
flush away any bad memory

Can you start seeds
from every plant
to regenerate new life

Can you step softly

Say the sunset over
the mountains
the orange pink scrim
over purple shaded
rocks is your favorite
daily entertainment

Can you say that rising
in gray darkness before the
sun is a strategy to survival

Do we not all have some
sort of bravery in us
what we learned ourselves

and what was given to
us freely on those walks
in 105 degree heat

I mean to share to
that type of courage

to say "listen
before judgment"

to defy blinding fear
deadly as 110 degree heat

and to trick yourself into stepping
forward even when
you don't know if there
is a road ahead of you

Susan Terence
Poet Teacher, San Francisco

My California

I come from rows plowed in dense soil
like lines in a poem, repeated and ordered
concealing what is germinating underneath. I am
from coastal June fog, summer clouds that droop to say hello
and gingko tree lined streets, from ice plant and juniper,
easily grown, long-lived, nondescript and green.
I am from pesticides sprayed on lettuce crops and the plume
from the Nestle chocolate factory, from so much
poison and magic in the morning air.
I am from the bougainvillea climbing trellises
with their pink blooming arms, and pots of red
geraniums on porches, in every mild season, stretching
their necks for a few more minutes of sun.
I am from endless fields of artichokes and iceberg lettuce,
from eucalyptus groves dropping woody seed pods
that look like oxidized ancient coins. I am from orphans
and immigrants, from ranch dust, almonds orchards,
chicken wire and poisoned blood in the central valley,
and from babies who felt the 1918 San Francisco Earthquake.
I am an aftershock.

I am also from cedar pollen that yellows the yard
in a such a thick way Van Gogh's palette would be jealous,
and from stacked Yuba River rocks, rooted in the rapids
I am from all the pink volunteer dogwood trees, dear trampled
pine needle trails, and the neighborhood crows
who are still trying to learn my name. I am from
late spring snow that breaks birch branches, but fills
reservoirs, from the hidden hives of honeybees and
the lavender they dance in. I am from the Virginia
Creeper vines winding through the cracked headstones
of pioneer cemeteries. I am from the clearest
midnight sky, at the end of my street, where

the stars forget there are cities always trying to
outshine them, and even though the shimmering
we see is already 10,000 years old, it seems
they still want to perform right now, arranging themselves in
a luminous tableau vivant. I know I am
not alone under these California constellations,
but tonight, it seems they are just for me.

Kirsten Casey
Poet Teacher, Nevada County

Building a Wall

Build a wall made of dusk and old saguaro lace,
sew it with threads of tumbleweed and twilight.
Then weave it into a net to catch the errant stars
as they cross from one no man's land into another,
marking that liminal shore, where the voices of dreams
become tangible, where the ragged mouth of time
bends to its own vagaries. Tells us stories of the old ways.
A wall, where the past and the future merge
into a shoreline where it is always now. No borders.
Nothing is written in stone. The old stories of sand
at river mouths whisper a journey of unimagined time.
Let the river touch the sea until sea and sky become one.
Call off the coyotes and let the voices of the wind
travel through razor wire, and border crossings
unimpeded by politics and greed. We are all immigrants
traveling to one promised land or another.
Make it not a wailing wall. Make it a singing wall
filled with the wings of prayer rags, and the gods of hope,
where the vagaries of war smoldering on battlefields
and contested borders becomes a thing of the past,
where the politics of religion no longer divide us,
and we move free as the clouds on the horizon.

Maureen Hurley
Poet Teacher, Alameda and Sonoma Counties

Town of Enfield on the Quabbin Reservoir

i danced for a ghost town
the water watched idly
lapping its applause
over the memory of life
underneath all this wilderland
a hundred years ago - evacuated
no, fled (or were forced to...)
and their homes became paper boats
the post-office packages floated
like bath toys
and their days were promised
to continue – elsewhere

i made a promise once
to myself
that i would try not to flood
the only body carrying me
its water an elixir
for everything that had gone wrong

so between these trees, i thought
all is well with me
but here i am at the foot
of a liquid cemetery
on the banks of stories
whose tellers drift aimless
through the fog
or else they've already ended
their lives
in search of a town
that looks over the lake

in hopes the church spires
still peek out
like buoys on the waves

Maxine Flasher-Düzgüneş
Poet Teacher, Marin County

Every Mother Mothers

"Good moms let you lick the beaters after making brownies,
great moms turn them off first."

She is our first home
first shelter, original refuge
drifting in the warm ocean of her life
her heartbeat guides ours into form
everything she is
becomes us
and we live on with her
embedded in our bones

like it or not
we are it
this sweet swift passage of time
from helpless to human
tiny creature to grown up
happens because she shared
her body
her freedom
her tenderness

Mothers of the world
we are here now
because of you
eating dainty sandwiches without crusts
and holding our cups out to the world
letting them fill over because you brought us here
gave us a chance to survive
to thrive
become a reflection
of the vastness of life's choices

Mothers, mothers, mothers
we all have them

---

some of us are them
others are in awe of them
none of us could
be here without our mothers

I for one
am grateful
for the trillions of women
who've passed time's torch
of imperative calling
to bring forth, nurture, protect, stand firm
fall down, get up
sing in the long tones of earth
dance in rainbow bands of light
dream galaxies into their wombs

whether it is animal fur and clay pots
or iphones and soccer games
mom's mirror the meaning of altruism
relinquishing self for other
finding compassion in empty wells
is in the contract
it's signed with blood

So the next time a mom asks if you want advice
remember it is a rhetorical question
and say yes
just say yes
and yes and yes and yes
open your arms, your heart
to the cord
that binds us all
to the love
that is
her home

Blake More
Poet Teacher, Mendocino County

I Write

I write
not knowing where the words,
gossamer winged,
might take me,
thorns or thistles,
to bleed or perch
upon their purple heady heights.
Nor can I, at best, predict
how long or short
their flight.
I can only follow,
stay true to how they lead,
pool to incandescent pool
into the dark,
returning to the aquifer
from which they spring
without pressing
to reach conscience's light
or out to senseless shining sea,
the wordless night
from which we come
and, at last, return.
I can only follow,
blind as Charon,
to wherever they may lead.

Jabez W. Churchill
Poet Teacher, Mendocino County

Recess

All they wanted was to run jump   push each other over
and pull each other up   outside on cold windy days
on the playground   to dive into the soft mattress
of grass and bounce back   even as adults watched warily
shaking their heads   concerned that one might shove
a little too hard   fall dangerously   break an arm if they
didn't settle them down   provide rules   special uniforms
make-up games they could supervise   referee   dividing
the children neatly into red and yellow teams
so one team could keep the ball away from the other
score points   and win   and later the adults invented
toddler soccer practice: pint-sized athletes kicking
small blue balls around   guided by middle aged men
in backward baseball caps, whistles dangling
from their necks who yelled out instructions for kicking
as the youngest kids sat or rolled on the grass
And once the toddlers grew older, the adults
carefully sectioned them off into appropriate sports
assigned corresponding equipment and rules
so later, some got to stand in left or right field
with their gloves poised mid-air waiting
for a ball to fly in their direction

Yet even after years of socialization and scheduled
practices, this afternoon when the bell rang for recess,
out poured a rush of exuberant boys and girls
running crazily in circles pulling pushing
climbing on friends throwing them down
onto the soft grass where they rolled together
then sprang up like testosterone charged
wildflowers straight
into air

Claire Blotter
Poet Teacher, Marin County

California Poets in the Schools

Collection Day

[Pandemic]

We are feeling the universe with giant
gloves which grow each night covering

the cosmos, as one covers their face
when caught by surprise or an overwhelming

grief. Cloud-shadows move and don't
move; walking trees make their way

closer to stars while we sleep, draped
on limbs. From the window I watch

a woman wheel a dog in a carriage on
the sidewalk as a man pushes a shopping

cart down the middle of the dead end
street. She's shouting at him across the space

between them, over the rattle of the metal
cart piled with plastic garbage bags full

of empties. They vanish from view, become
barely audible: gone. I put on my mask

and go outside. After collection, blue
recycling bins stand like bodies gathered

for an action yet to begin. I breathe through
the tight weave, watch the light salvage

wreckage from the sun; I am too seldom
at the ocean to hear the murmuring of shells.

Virginia Barrett
Poet Teacher, Marin County

The Messenger Prince

It understands the braille of water,
drinking through its skin,
so delicate you can't handle it
without contaminating
the creature.

The frog so permeable,
to pesticides,
        detergents,
                fertilizers.
The amphibian in the coal mine
of any habitat blitzed
by pollution.

200 frog species vanished
in the last 40 years.

They are a membrane away
from our own skin,
already a prince
before our kiss—
a messenger, a savior
if we just pay attention to
their song growing fainter and fainter
along lakes,
swamps, riverbanks.

Terri Glass
Poet Teacher, Marin & Del Norte Counties

Acknowledgements:

We rely upon the generosity of the community to advance our mission and vision. California Poets in the Schools would like to thank the following sponsors for helping to make the 2023-2024 poetry anthology possible:

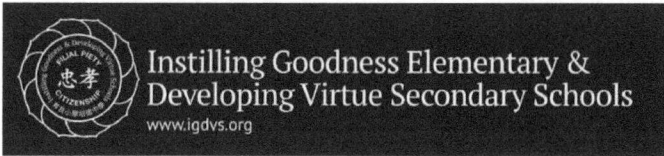

Instilling Goodness Developing Virtue School

The Jai Chandra Singh Foundation JCSF

About California Poets in the Schools

Now in our 60th year, California Poets in the Schools has grown to become one of the oldest and largest writers-in-the-schools programs in the nation. Our reach includes 15,000 students served annually by 70 Poet-Teachers from throughout California. Poet-Teachers live and serve students K-12 in over 30 California counties, stretching from Humboldt and Siskiyou to Los Angeles and San Diego, in districts both urban and rural. Each year California Poets in the Schools' Poet-Teachers reach hundreds of classrooms, teaching in public and private schools, juvenile halls, after-school programs, hospitals and other community settings. California Poets in the Schools champions and amplifies the voices of California youth by providing platforms for critical literacy, youth development and leadership through school-based poetry writing, publication and performance opportunities.

California Poets in the Schools' vision is to enable youth in every California county to discover, cultivate and amplify their own creative voices through reading, analyzing, writing, performing and publishing poetry. When students learn to express their creativity, imagination, and intellectual curiosity through poetry, it becomes a catalyst for learning core academic subjects, accelerating emotional development and supporting personal growth. Poet-Teachers help students become adults who will bring compassion, understanding and appreciation for diverse perspectives both in and outside the classroom.

California Poets in the Schools develops and empowers a multicultural network of independent Poet-Teachers, who bring the many benefits of poetry to youth throughout the state. As a membership network we offer opportunities for professional development, peer learning and fundraising assistance for Poet-Teachers in California. We also cultivate relationships with school districts, foundations and arts organizations which can fund and support our members' professional practices.

Learn more at www.cpits.org
Contact us at info@cpits.org

California Poets IN THE SCHOOLS

60TH ANNIVERSARY

California Poets in the Schools is a 501(c)3 organization.
Funding for this 60th Anniversary Anthology comes 100% from
individuals and small businesses. We rely upon the generosity of
the community to advance our mission and vision. A donation
to our organization helps us to inspire more young people to
find their unique voices through poetry, while expanding the
audience for poetry. If you are interested in sponsoring next
year's anthology, please reach out at info@cpits.org.

Donate today at www.californiapoets.org.

Milton Keynes UK
Ingram Content Group UK Ltd.
UKHW040056151124
2855UKWH00068B/171

9 780939 927326